Further Ahead

A communication skills course
for Business English

Home Study Book

Sarah Jones-Macziola

CAMBRIDGE
UNIVERSITY PRESS

PUBLISHED BY THE PRESS SYNDICATE OF THE UNIVERSITY OF CAMBRIDGE
The Pitt Building, Trumpington Street, Cambridge, United Kingdom

CAMBRIDGE UNIVERSITY PRESS
The Edinburgh Building, Cambridge CB2 2RU, UK
40 West 20th Street, New York, NY 10011–4211, USA
477 Williamstown Road, Port Melbourne, VIC 3207, Australia
Ruiz de Alarcón 13, 28014 Madrid, Spain
Dock House, The Waterfront, Cape Town 8001, South Africa

http://www.cambridge.org

First published 1999
Fourth printing 2002

Printed in the United Kingdom at the University Press, Cambridge

ISBN 0 521 59783 8   Home Study Book
ISBN 0 521 59782 X   Home Study Cassette
ISBN 0 521 63929 8   Home Study CD
ISBN 0 521 59784 6   Teacher's Guide
ISBN 0 521 59786 2   Learner's Book
ISBN 0 521 59785 4   Learner's Book Cassette
ISBN 0 521 63928 X   Learner's Book CD
ISBN 0 521 58779 4   Video and Teacher's Guide (VHS PAL)
ISBN 0 521 58778 6   Video and Teacher's Guide (VHS SECAM)
ISBN 0 521 58777 8   Video and Teacher's Guide (VHS NTSC)
ISBN 0 521 62645 5   Video Activity Book

Contents

Acknowledgements

The authors and publishers are grateful to the following copyright owners for permission to reproduce copyright material. Every endeavour has been made to contact copyright owners and apologies are expressed for any omissions.

p. 3 Nihon Keizai Shimbun, Inc; p. 4 Teva Pharmaceutical Industries, Ltd; p. 5 "A gift for Business" first published in *Business Life*, November 1996; pp. 12 and 43 "Time on their hands" and "A question of culture" © The Economist; p. 16 Railfreight Distribution; p. 20 Great North Eastern Railway; p. 26 *Financial Times*. 19.10.1993; pp. 29 and 34 Arjo Wiggins Fine Papers Ltd; pp. 30, 34, 39, 51, The Independent/Independent on Sunday; p. 33 Hyundai Car (UK) Ltd.

The authors and publishers are grateful to the following illustrators and photographic sources:

pp. 1, 26 and 39, © Pictor International; p. 2 © Spectrum Colour Library / D and J Heaton; p. 5 Spectrum Colour Library; p. 3 Laurence Hunter; p. 15 Photostock / Charles Tyler; p. 16 Railfreight Distribution; p. 19 © The Image Bank / Guido Alberto Rossi; p. 20 *l* National Railway Museum / Science and Society; p. 20 *r* ©The Image Bank; p. 29 Samsung; p. 33 Hyundai Car (UK) Ltd; p. 40 ©Britstock-IFA / ICS Fabricius-Taylor; p. 40 © Hulton Getty; p. 43 © Alison Wright / Panos; p. 46 Stena Lines; p. 48 © Powerstock; p. 50 Nike (UK) Ltd; p.51 Volvo Car UK Limited.

How to use the *Further Ahead Home Study Book*

The *Further Ahead Home Study Book* has many activities for you to do at home. There are:
- exercises to practise grammar and vocabulary from the *Learner's Book*
- extra listening, reading and writing tasks
- test units to help you check your progress.

Answers to most of the exercises are in the key at the back of the book. Some exercises have no key, so compare your answers with another learner or ask your teacher to check them.

Each unit has three sections; you need about twenty minutes to do a section or an hour for each unit.

Each unit has listening activities in which you will hear speakers in different business situations.

There are complete tapescripts of all the listening tasks in the key. You can use these to check your answers or if you cannot understand something.

1 People

1 Language in use

You are talking to someone at a conference. Make questions about the words in *italics* in their answers like this:

1 A: What's your name?

B: My name's *Choong-Su Lee*.

2 A: ....

B: I'm a *plastics engineer*.

3 A: ....

B: I work for *Nyltech*.

4 A: ....

B: I'm from *Seoul*.

5 A: ....

B: I live in *Paris*.

2 Language in use

Match a phrase in column A to a phrase in column B like this:

A	B
1 How are things?	a How do you do?
2 Do you know Dave Thomas?	b Fine, thanks.
3 Pleased to meet you.	c And I'm Paolo.
4 Please call me Dave.	d No, I don't think we've met before.
5 Have you met Rosa Barea?	e Yes, I have. Good to see you again, Rosa.

3 Language in use

Put these sentences in the correct order to form a conversation.

☐ How are things at head office?

☐ Hello, Michael, I'm fine thanks. How are you?

☐ Yes, thanks, although it was a little rough.

☐ Hello, Andrea, how are you?

☐ We've been really busy, I think we're going to have a very good year!

☐ Not too bad. Did you have a good flight?

Now listen to the conversation and check your answers.

1

1.2 Keeping the conversation going

① Language in use

Match a phrase in column A to a phrase in column B like this:

A	B
1 What do you think of the conference?	a At Shepheard's Hotel.
2 Which part of Egypt are you from?	b Yes, I visited a factory there last year.
3 Where are you staying?	c It's very interesting.
4 Have you been to our Bombay office?	d No, I don't. I work at the office in Alexandria.
5 Do you work here in Cairo?	e Asyut. It's in the south.

② Language in use

You are talking to a visitor to your company. Make questions like this:

1 A: Hello, Roberto. It's nice to see you again. How are you?

B: Fine, thanks.

2 A: ....

B: Yesterday evening, at about 7 o'clock.

3 A: ....

B: At the Hilton. It's very central.

4 A: ....

B: No. It's such a nice day that I walked to the office.

5 A: ....

B: Three days. I'm flying to Rio on Thursday.

6 A: ....

B: A coffee would be nice.

③ ▭ ◎ Listening

Listen to this conversation. What is wrong with it?
Now write a better version of it.

A: ....

B: ....

A: ....

B: ....

A: ....

B: ....

A: ....

B: ....

1.3 Finding out about people

❶ Reading

Read the text below and decide if these statements are true (T) or false (F).

1 The *Nikkei Weekly* is written in Japanese. ☐

2 It reports stories from American newspapers and magazines. ☐

3 Nikkei is a large publisher. ☐

4 Three million people read the *Nikkei Weekly*. ☐

Do you want to know what the Japanese are thinking?

Then read what they're reading. Every week the *Nikkei Weekly* reports in English all the major stories appearing in the Japanese business newspapers and magazines. You get the same news the Japanese are getting. The *Nikkei Weekly* is published by Nikkei, the number one business publisher in Japan. Nikkei publishes many business newspapers and magazines including the *Nihon Keizai Shimbun*, which has a circulation of 3,000,000. Through these publications, Nikkei gives the Japanese people the news and views that shape what they are thinking. If you want to know what the Japanese are thinking, read the *Nikkei Weekly*.

❷ Grammar

Match a phrase in column A to a phrase in column B like this:

A	B
1 That man with the glasses is Andrew Cheng,	a don't they?
2 The woman next to him isn't Susie Yang,	b does she?
	c isn't it?
3 They work for Asia Motors,	d isn't he?
4 He's the Sales Director,	e was he?
5 She doesn't live here,	f is it?
6 He wasn't at the fair last year,	

❸ 📼 ◎ Listening

Listen to the conversation and tick (✓) the sentences that are true.

1 Vikkie Behle still works for the company. ☐

2 Carol Simms took Vikkie's job. ☐

3 Carol never worked at Jones's. ☐

4 Carol worked at Lear's many years ago. ☐

5 Vikkie and Carol have never met. ☐

2 Talking about companies

2.1 Describing a company

① Reading

Read this company profile and answer the questions.

Teva Pharmaceutical Industries is one of Israel's leading pharmaceutical companies. It has manufacturing facilities and marketing networks at home and abroad.

More than 50 per cent of Teva's sales are to overseas markets, primarily the United States. Teva manufactures a wide range of pharmaceutical products, including drugs used in many famous brands. Teva is also Israel's largest manufacturer and distributor of veterinary products and hospital supplies.

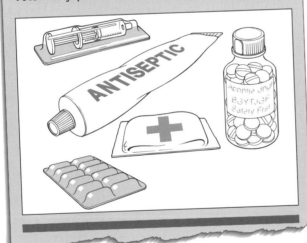

1 What type of business is Teva in?

....

2 What does it do?

....

3 Where is its main market?

....

② Language in use

You are talking to someone about their company. Make questions about the words in *italics* in their answers like this:

1 A: *Who do you work for?*

B: I work for *Calloway Golf*.

2 A: ....

B: We're in the *sports business*.

3 A: ....

B: We make *golf clubs*.

4 A: ....

B: Our headquarters are in *California*.

5 A: ....

B: Our main markets are in the *USA*.

6 A: ....

B: We employ about *2,000* people.

③ Writing

Complete these sentences. Use your own information or write about a company you would like to work for.

1 I work for ....

2 We're in the .... business.

3 We make ....

4 Our headquarters are in ....

5 Our main markets are in ....

6 We employ ....

2.2 Starting a business

1 ☰ ⊙ Listening

Listen to Annoushka Ducus talking about her career and match the date to an event.

1 1984   a   went to Paris to learn French
2 1985   b   her mother died
3 1986   c   sold the fish business
4 1988   d   did a secretarial course
5 1989   e   opened a sandwich bar in Brisbane
6 1994   f   took over the fish business

2 Grammar

Here is the past tense of some common irregular verbs. Write the base form.

1 .... was / were   7 .... had
2 .... became   8 .... left
3 .... began   9 .... made
4 .... did   10 .... said
5 .... got   11 .... sold
6 .... went   12 .... took

3 Vocabulary

Match an adjective to a noun.

1 main   a   turnover
2 regional   b   office
3 annual   c   branches

Match a verb to a noun.

4 set up   d   staff
5 make   e   a company
6 employ   f   goods

Now complete these sentences using some of the above expressions.

7 Our .... is in London.

8 We have an .... of over £4 million.

9 Last year we opened two .... in the United States.

10 We .... 80 ....

2.3 Getting product information

❶ Reading and writing

Read this reply to a letter of enquiry. Then write the letter Mr Koh sent. Look at the *Learner's Book* if you need help.

ELECTROSTIR
Orchard Street, Ashford, Kent TN10 1AH
Tel: 01233 339555
Fax: 01233 339556
E-mail: gwinter@electrostir.com
Web: www.electrostir.com

Mr H. Koh
17 Glendale Road
Glasgow G14 1RU
Scotland

1 December 199-

Dear Mr Koh

Thank you for your letter of 21 November 199- enquiring about our products.

We have pleasure in enclosing our latest catalogue together with details of prices. Please note that we offer a 10% discount for orders placed before 31 January.

If you need any further information, please contact me.

Yours sincerely

Gail Winter

Enc. catalogue, price list

❷ 🔌 ◎ Listening

Listen to two people calling Electrostir and write down their addresses.

Call 1

Louise Nevelson
....
....
....

Call 2

Simon Wright
....
....
....
....

❸ Language in use

Complete this telephone call like this:

1 A: Electrostir, Sales Department.
    Good morning.

  B: This is Kavita Choudhry from RRL in India. I'm interested in your range of magnetic stirrers. Could you send me some literature?

2 A: ....
  B: My name's Choudhry.

3 A: ....
  B: Choudhry. Kavita Choudhry.

4 A: ....
  B: Yes, that's C.H.O.U.D.H.R.Y.

5 A: ....
  B: Sure, it's RRL. You have our address on file.

6 A: ....
  B: Thank you very much.

3 Jobs

3.1 Company structure

① Vocabulary

Match a word in column A to a word or expression in column B like this:

A	B
1 leading	a applicant
2 keyboard	b manner
3 telephone	c salary
4 attractive	d suppliers
5 pleasant	e skills
6 successful	f work environment

Now complete the blanks in the advertisement using some of the expressions above.

Secretary to the Export Sales Manager

We are one of the .... ⁽⁷⁾ of tractor parts.

We are looking for a Secretary for the Export Sales Manager.

The .... ⁽⁸⁾ will have: excellent .... ⁽⁹⁾ and a working knowledge of Spanish and French.

In return we offer an .... ⁽¹⁰⁾ and 6 weeks' holiday.

Please write for an application form.
Human Resources Officer
Massey Robertson
Willowdale
Ontario M5X 1B4
Canada

② Writing

Read this letter and put the missing phrases in the right place.

> **a** word processing programs
> **b** hearing from you
> **c** I am working as a Secretary
> **d** the position
> **e** fluent Spanish and French
> **f** Secretary to the Export Sales Manager

22 June 199-

Dear Sir or Madam

I have seen your advertisement for a .... ⁽¹⁾ in *The Globe and Mail* and would like to apply for .... ⁽²⁾.

I am 33 years old and at present .... ⁽³⁾ in the Sales Department at Continental Assurance. I am familiar with common .... ⁽⁴⁾ and I speak .... ⁽⁵⁾. Further information is in my CV.

I look forward to .... ⁽⁶⁾.

Yours sincerely,

S. Blaggs

③ Vocabulary

Use these clues to complete the word grid.

1 Sales representatives do this.
2 Payment for work.
3 Person who works in an office.
4 Company cars are an example of these.
5 Head of a company in the USA.
6 To ask for a job in writing.
7 Job not filled.

3.2 Describing responsibilities

❶ Grammar

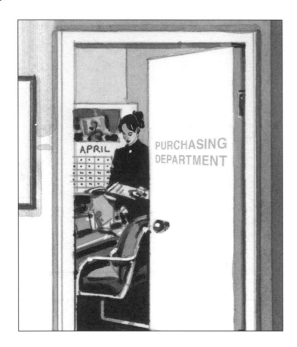

Study the verbs in this conversation. Label each one 'E' or 'T' according to this key: E = activities which happen again and again or all the time; T = temporary activities or activities happening 'around now'.

A: Which department do you work [(1)] in?

B: I usually work [(2)] in the Purchasing department, but today I'm helping [(3)] in the Marketing department.

A: What do you do [(4)] in the Purchasing department?

B: I buy [(5)] anything that is needed for the office. I also check [(6)] that we purchase [(7)] goods at the lowest prices. At the moment, we're having [(8)] problems with one of our suppliers. They are delivering [(9)] goods late and are charging [(10)] more for their products. I'm looking [(11)] for a new supplier!

1	E	2	....	3	....	4	....
5	....	6	....	7	....	8	....
9	....	10	....	11	....		

❷ Grammar

Complete the paragraph below using the correct tense of the verbs in the box.

help   send   answer   work   send   pack

I _work_ [(1)] in the Dispatch department.

We .... [(2)] goods to customers. At the moment we're very busy because we

.... [(3)] machines for a trade fair next week.

   This is my colleague. She .... [(4)] in the Export department. She .... [(5)] customers' enquiries about our products and

.... [(6)] them information. This week she .... [(7)] me prepare for the fair.

🔲 ◉

Now listen and check your answers.

❸ Writing

Complete these sentences about yourself. Use your own information or write about a job you would like to do.

1 I work in the .... department.

2 I'm responsible for ....

3 I also ....

4 At the moment I ....

3.3 Leaving a message

1 Vocabulary

Match the caption to a picture.

a She's on holiday.
b There's no reply.
c He's at lunch.
d She's in a meeting.
e The line's engaged.
f He's sick.

2 🔲 ◎ Listening

Listen and complete the messages.

Call 1

For: ....

From: ....

Message: ....

....

....

....

Call 2

For: ....

From: ....

Message: ....

....

....

....

3 Language in use

Complete this telephone call like this:

1 A: Accounts department. Good morning.

   B: Could I speak to Jeremy Tan, please?

2 A: ....

   ....

   B: Do you know when it will finish?

3 A: ....

   ....

   B: Could you ask him to call me about the invoice he sent me, please?

4 A: ....

   ....

   B: My name's Salcini. Lisa Salcini.

5 A: ....

   ....

   B: It's 777 1722.

6 A: ....

   ....

   B: Thank you very much. Goodbye.

4 Work and play

4.1 Inviting

❶ Reading

Read the text below. Decide in which country or countries business people invite guests to do the following:

a go to the theatre
b watch a tennis match
c go sailing
d visit an art exhibition.

WHAT TO EXPECT ON THAT TRIP TO EUROPE:
A business entertaining guide

ITALY: Art is among the most favoured corporate entertainments and big companies such as Fiat organize exhibitions complete with the services of an art historian to guide clients on private previews.

FRANCE: Good food is naturally the principal preoccupation. Among sports events, the French Open tennis and the horse racing at Chantilly rate highly.

GERMANY: A free trip to a holiday spot is a frequent perk. Sports events are also popular, particularly the German Open tennis and the Grand Prix at Hockenheim. Munich's beer festival is another well-known event visitors might be invited to.

SPAIN: If you are a shooting enthusiast, you might be offered a weekend with wild boar and partridge shooting in the country. Your hosts are unlikely to offer to take you to the bullfights unless you show a keen interest.

HOLLAND: Gifts of gold are a popular business perk in the Netherlands. But some Dutch companies like to take clients sailing on the Ijsselmeer or hire boats to show them picturesque villages such as Monnickendam.

GREECE: A cruise to the islands is popular in warm weather, as is going to a theatrical performance at the ancient theatre at Epidavrus.

---

❷ 🔈 ◎ Listening and speaking

Practise inviting your business partner out. Study this example, then make invitations based on the prompts you will hear.

VOICE 1: dinner tonight (*beep*)

YOU: Would you like to have dinner tonight?

VOICE 2: Would you like to have dinner tonight? (*repeat*)

❸ Language in use

Complete the following dialogues.

1 A: I hear you play tennis. Would you like a game this evening?

  B: I'm afraid I'm ....

  ....

  A: That's a pity. How about tomorrow evening?

  B: ....

  ....

2 A: Would you like to watch a game of German football? Dortmund is playing Bayern München on Saturday.

  B: ....

  ....

  A: It starts at three. I'll pick you up at your hotel.

  B: ....

  ....

4.2 Getting to know you

1 Vocabulary

Put these words into categories.

> novel   biography   classical   western
> jazz   horror   comedy   soul
> science fiction   pop   crime   thriller

Books	Films	Music
....	....	....
....	....	....
....	....	....
....	....	....

Now complete these sentences.

1 The last book I read was a ....

2 The last film I saw was a ....

3 I like listening to .... music,

   but I'm not very keen on ....

   music.

2 Writing

Put these jumbled sentences into the correct order to form a dialogue.

a ☐ No, I don't really like films. But I do enjoy reading, and I agree with you about thrillers!

b ☐ Yes. After a hard day in the office there's nothing better than a good game of tennis! What about you? Do you like sports?

c ☐ Oh. What sort of films do you like?

d ☐ So, Sarah, I understand that you play a lot of sports in your free time?

e ☐ I really like thrillers, something with a bit of excitement. Do you like going to the cinema?

f ☐ I'm afraid I don't. I like swimming, but I don't have much time. However, I do like going to the cinema.

3 Writing

Complete these sentences about yourself.

1 In my free time I

2 I like

                                   ,

   but I don't like

3 I don't really like

4 I'm quite interested in

5 I'm not really interested in

6 My favourite way of spending time is to

4.3 Market research

Listen and fill in the missing figures.

TIME ON THEIR HANDS

Europeans work fewer hours for more money. So what do they do with their time? In the cold, grey north they watch TV. Denmark has .... (1) sets for every 1,000 people, Germany has .... (2). In sunny Spain they eat out: .... (3) of household spending goes on restaurants, cafés and hotels.

Europeans everywhere watch football. One in .... (4) is interested in football, one in .... (5) in tennis and swimming and one in .... (6) in athletics and gymnastics.

Above all, the newly rich Europeans go on holiday. .... (7) take their main holidays in August and another .... (8) in July. For peace (if not sun) try February or November, when only .... (9) take their main holiday. .... (10) of Europe's holidaymakers head for the seaside. But in Holland people prefer a holiday in the countryside to a week on the beach.

❷ Reading

Read the article again and answer these questions.

1 What do Northern Europeans do in their free time?
2 What do Southern Europeans do in their free time?
3 What is the most popular sport in Europe?
4 What other sports are Europeans interested in?
5 When do most Europeans take their holidays?
6 Where do they like to spend their holidays?

❸ Grammar

Put these words on the line below in order of frequency.

never often usually sometimes frequently regularly seldom

↑   ↑   ↑   ↑   ↑   ↑   ↑

always

Now complete these sentences about yourself with words from the box.

1 I .... watch television in the evening.
2 I .... go out to eat.
3 I .... play football and I .... play tennis.
4 I .... take my main holiday in July or August.
5 I .... take my main holiday in February or November.
6 I .... go to the seaside for my holiday.

Progress test 1

5.1 Grammar

Complete these sentences with the correct form of the verb in (brackets).

Nicole .... (*work*) (1) in the Marketing department of a large toy manufacturer. She .... (*answer*) (2) customer enquiries, ... (*deal*) (3) with complaints and .... (*prepare*) (4) catalogues. Today she .... (*prepare*) (5) for an exhibition. She .... (*organize*) (6) everything and .... (*write*) (7) a short presentation.

5.2 Vocabulary

Complete the sentences using the words or expressions in the box below.

annual turnover   main office   employs staff
leading supplier   regional branches

Megabyte is a .... (1) of computer hardware. Its .... (2) is in London, and 12 .... (3) cover the UK. It .... 80 .... (4) and has an .... (5) in excess of £81 million.

5.3 Grammar

Add question tags to complete these sentences.

1 You know Barbara Hull,

.... ?

2 She works at Excel,

.... ?

3 Her husband is a bank manager,

.... ?

4 They live in Glasgow,

.... ?

5 She doesn't work for Comco now,

.... ?

5.4 Language in use

Here is your diary for this week. Today is Monday. A colleague phones to invite you out. Complete the conversation below.

MONDAY
Evening: client dinner

TUESDAY
To Rome 8 a.m., return 10 p.m.

WEDNESDAY

THURSDAY

FRIDAY
Mother's birthday party

FRIEND: Would you ....

.... (tonight)?

YOU: I'm afraid ....

FRIEND: ....
....
(tomorrow night)?

YOU: I'm sorry ....
....

How about ....
(Thursday evening)?

FRIEND: Thursday would be fine. ....
.... (7 o'clock)?

YOU: Seven o'clock would be fine. I'll see you
then. Bye for now.

FRIEND: Bye.

5.5 Grammar

Complete these sentences with the correct form of the verb in (brackets).

Monterrey Taco Company ....
(*begin*) [1] business in 1978 and quickly

.... (*become*) [2] a successful

company. It .... (*start*) [3] with
the simple idea of selling high quality food at low
prices and in pleasant surroundings. In its first year

it .... (*make*) [4] a good profit.

In 1980 it .... (*take*) [5] over
another small Tex–Mex chain, and in 1989 it

.... (*sell*) [6] its millionth meal.

5.6 ▭ ◉ Listening

Listen to the phone call and complete the message pad below.

Message

To: ....

From: ....

Message: ....

....

....

....

....

....

6 Transportation

6.1 Describing infrastructure

1 Reading

Look at this advertisement for Singapore and fill in the correct headings from the box below.

> **a** Living standards **b** Communications
> **c** Transport **d** Human resources
> **e** Commercial premises **f** Services

Is this why 3,000 global companies have chosen Singapore?

1 ....
World's top airport (rated by *Business Traveller*) and busiest seaport.

2 ....
Workers rated amongst the world's best for attitude, productivity and technical skills.

3 ....
Modern and reliable telecommunication services at the most competitive rates.

4 ....
Well developed supporting industry with a wide range of competitively priced quality parts and services.

5 ....
Ready built factories, fully serviced industrial parks and modern office space.

6 ....
Safe, modern cosmopolitan city offering excellent living conditions.

2 Listening

Listen to an interview with an executive discussing what she looks for when considering where to locate an office. Put the following points in the order she mentions them.

a ☐ Communications
b ☐ Services
c ☐ Commercial premises
d ☐ Living standards
e ☐ Human resources
f ☐ Transport

3 Vocabulary

Use the following transport terms to complete the paragraph below.

> airport   cargo ship   goods trains
> lorry   rail   port   container

Moving goods around the world is an important business today. How you send them depends on a number of factors.

If speed is important, it is usually possible to send or receive goods at your local .... (1). Many specialist companies have their own fleets of aircraft and can transport goods world-wide.

If you are sending large quantities of goods, then there are several options. On land, you can send goods by .... (2) on special .... (3). You can also send goods by .... (4) using the road system.

The .... (5) system offers great flexibility. Goods are loaded into special boxes which can be transferred from one form of transport to another without ever being opened. A modern .... (6) will have facilities for loading these boxes direct from .... (7) to rail or lorry, depending on what is most efficient.

1 Reading

Read the advertisement below. Are these statements true (T) or false (F)?

1 Railfreight Distribution carries freight from Britain to Europe. ☐

2 It takes 32 hours to take freight from Manchester to Milan by road. ☐

3 More companies are using rail since the Channel Tunnel opened. ☐

4 Railfreight has invested a lot of money to improve services. ☐

Europe's future is on the line

With no road congestion, no port hold-ups and no problems with bad weather, Railfreight Distribution offers the fast way to transport freight across the Channel. In addition, our services are safe, flexible and environmentally friendly. Together with our European partners, we provide a network of freight services across the Continent. This makes it possible to send goods from Milan to Manchester in 32 hours, a whole day faster than by road.

Since the Channel Tunnel opened, more and more companies have turned to rail for their distribution requirements. We have also invested over £400 million to deliver even faster and more economical services. So whether your business is new cars, domestic electrical equipment, steel, food and drink products, textiles or furniture (to name but a few), Railfreight Distribution can put your business on a direct line to Europe.

2 Language in use

You work for a company that ships goods within Europe. Compare Railfreight Distribution to other forms of transportation and make sentences like this:

1 reliable / air
   Rail is more reliable than air transport.

2 road / safe
   ....

3 fast / road
   ....

4 flexible / sea
   ....

5 economical / air
   ....

3 Vocabulary

Use these clues to complete the word grid.

1 Farm animals such as cattle and sheep.
2 Goods that burn easily are ... .
3 Goods that go bad quickly are ... .
4 Delicate goods are ... .
5 Dangerous goods are ... .
6 Goods transported by plane or ship.

6.3 Dealing with an order

❶ 📼 ◎ Listening

You are Brian Davison at VAC Industries. Listen to this voice mail message and complete the order form below.

V A C
Industries

28 Devon Road, Plymouth PL1 1HZ
Fax: ++44 (0) 1752 323821
Tel: ++44 (0) 1752 328822

Order from: .... (1)

Time/Date: .... (2)

Items:

Units	Model
.... (3)	.... (4)
.... (5)	.... (6)

Delivery instructions

Send to: .... (7)

Company: .... (8)

Mode of shipment: .... (9)

Payment instructions

Goods: 60 days

Insurance: (Tick) Yes ☐   No ☐

Transport to be paid by: VAC ☐   Customer ☐

❷ Reading

You've just received this E-mail from Ms Sanchez. What changes does she want to make to her order?

To: Brian Davison
From: Ms Sanchez, Royale Engineering

I am sorry to have to make changes to this morning's order. We now require 3 units of model 1380 and 4 units of model 1935. Also, we now do not need them so urgently, so please send them by sea. As usual, you will pay for transport by sea.

❸ Writing

Now complete the following memo to the Dispatch department.

V A C
Industries

From: Brian Davison
To: Dispatch Department
Date: ....

Goods details

Units	Model
....	....
....	....

Shipping details

Please send ....
....
....
....

7 Imports and exports

7.1 Talking about industries

1 Reading

Label each paragraph with the correct country from the box.

| Brazil   Australia   Switzerland |

1 ....

World's largest wool producer, and a top exporter of veal and beef. The country's most important crop is wheat. Discoveries of petroleum reserves in the early 1960s have turned the country into a major oil producer. Commercial oil production began in 1964. The manufacturing industry has expanded rapidly since 1945, especially in engineering, shipbuilding, car manufacture, food processing and wine.

2 ....

Increased specialization in high-technology products, watches, drugs and chemicals; a major financial centre and headquarters of many international organizations; all-year-round tourist area.

3 ....

One of the world's largest farming countries, agriculture employs 35 per cent of the population; world's largest exporter of coffee; second largest exporter of cocoa and soya beans; steel, chemicals and motor vehicles.

2 ▭◎ Listening

Listen to this talk about the economy of Argentina and complete the following chart.

Total earnings

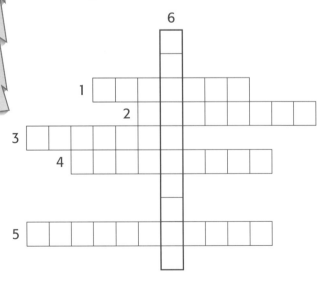

.... 6%

.... 63%

.... 31%

Listen again and complete these figures:

Exports (in billions of US$)

Fruit and vegetables: ....

Processed foods: ....

Livestock: ....

Minerals: ....

3 Vocabulary

Use these clues to complete the word grid.

1 This industry is involved in the manufacture of cloth.
2 This industry makes an electronic machine for storing and organizing information.
3 This industry brings in foreign visitors to see and enjoy a country and its sights.
4 This industry extracts a natural substance from the earth and turns it into a source of energy.
5 This industry grows our food.
6 This industry makes vehicles for personal transportation.

7.2 Talking about imports and exports

1 Language in use

You want some information about the goods Cuba imports. Make questions like this:

1 oil   How much oil do you import?

2 tractors

3 coffee

4 steel

5 textiles

6 wheat

2 Language in use

Look at this chart and make some sentences about these exports. Use the words in the box to help you.

| a lot of | much | many | some | a little | a few |

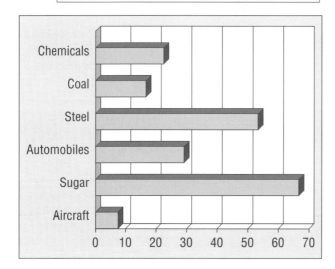

1   They export a few aircraft.

2

3

4

5

6

3 Writing

Look at the chart and complete the paragraph.

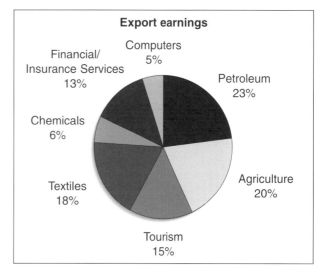

The largest export for this country is

.... [1], while the smallest is

.... [2]. Financial

and insurance services contribute .... [3],

and tourism contributes .... [4].

Fertile land and good rainfall, together with a

warm climate, make .... [5] a

major earner for the economy (.......... %) [6].

Suitable conditions for sheep and good

cotton-growing areas make .... [7]

the third largest contributor to the economy.

🔊 ⊚

Now listen and check your answers.

❶ Reading

Read this advertisement and answer the questions below.

The new golden age of rail travel is arriving

The days when to travel by rail was to travel in style are returning – in grand style. Already we have reduced fares between Scotland and London, put on more trains between Bradford and London, improved timekeeping and begun a multi-million pound improvement programme. Down the line are redesigned carriages, luxurious lounges and smart modern stations. At Great North Eastern Railway we look forward to your company on our exciting journey ahead.

---

1 Fares to Scotland are now

a more expensive.   b the same.
c cheaper.

2 Trains are

a less punctual.   b more punctual.
c less frequent.

3 GNER is investing

a a lot of money.
b a small amount of money.
c no money.

4 The number of trains between Bradford and London

a has decreased.   b has increased.
c has stayed the same.

❷ Grammar

Read this text about Taiwan and <u>underline</u> the correct tense in *italics*.

In the 1950s Taiwan <u>*was*</u> / *has been* [1] an agricultural country. Fifteen years ago the business world *knew* / *has known* [2] Taiwan as a source of cheap mass-produced goods. Since then there *was* / *has been* [3] a business revolution. Taiwanese companies *became* / *have become* [4] leaders in the field of hi-tech computer components. These firms *began* / *have begun* [5] investing in foreign countries. In the last 15 years the quality of Taiwanese goods *improved* / *has improved* [6].

❸ Writing

Write a short description based on the information below.

West Air

1988	1999
10 used aircraft	30 jet aircraft, all new
18 destinations	45 destinations
One class service	New business class introduced
No airport lounges	Start of programme to provide lounges in all major airports

In 1988 West Air started with 10 used aircraft. Today, it has expanded to 30 new jet aircraft.

....

....

....

8 Arrangements

1 Grammar

Read this memo and complete it using the verbs in the box below.

| fly | take | send | meet | go | phone |

To: Ellen
From: Michael
Re: James's visit to the London office

We .... (1) James on Monday, 1 August. He .... (2) to London from Edinburgh. I don't know the exact time of his flight. I .... (3) him to check the flight details. He hasn't received a copy of the report yet, so I .... (4) him one this afternoon. I .... (5) to Frankfurt that evening, so I .... (6) James to the airport for his return flight.

---

2 Listening and speaking

You are discussing a colleague's trip to visit your office. Unfortunately, the line is bad and you cannot hear very well. Study this example, then make questions based on the prompts you will hear.

VOICE 1: I'm arriving on ... (*beep*)

YOU: When are you arriving?

VOICE 2: When are you arriving? (*repeat*)

3 Language in use

Write a short description of your own schedule for tomorrow for work/school.

....
....
....
....
....
....
....
....

8.2 Dealing with correspondence

❶ Vocabulary

Match the verbs in column A to the nouns in column B like this:

A	B
1 enclose	a an appointment
2 make	b a conference
3 attend	c a table
4 book	d a registration form
5 reserve	e a reservation
6 confirm	f a room

Now complete this letter using some of the above expressions.

18 July 199-

Dear Emil

Thank you for your letter of 3 July

asking me to .... the

.... (7) in September of

this year. I .... my

.... (8). Please

.... (9) for four nights at

the nearest hotel.

I would like to meet Mr Paterson on the

second night of the conference. Please

.... (10) for two people in

the restaurant for that night.

❷ Language in use

Match the function on the left to the words you would use on the right.

1 inviting
2 accepting
3 confirming
4 arranging
5 cancelling
6 thanking

a I am pleased to confirm your meeting with Ms Smith ...

b Thank you for your hospitality while I was in Bangkok ...

c I will be pleased to attend the launch of your new range of ...

d Please book a room for the night of 27 July ...

e We are pleased to invite you to the launch of our new range ...

f I am afraid I will not be able to keep my appointment on ...

❸ Writing

You have just returned from a meeting. There are two notes on your desk. Write an appropriate letter to each of them.

1

Mr Howard called from Textile Import Ltd. He invited you to attend the launch of their new range on 13 February. Don't forget, however, that you have to travel to Paris that same evening.

2

Ms Smith from Infotel called to invite you to view their new range of software on Monday, 29 January. You are free that night.

8.3 Making and changing an appointment

1 ▭ ◉ Listening

Look at Paul's diary for next week. Listen to him discussing his appointments with a colleague and correct any mistakes.

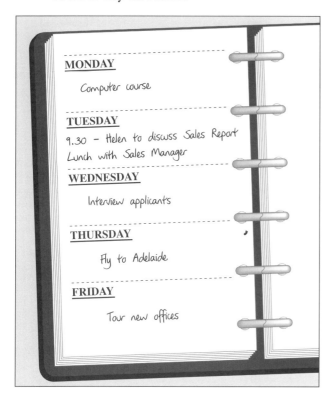

MONDAY

Computer course

TUESDAY

9.30 – Helen to discuss Sales Report
Lunch with Sales Manager

WEDNESDAY

Interview applicants

THURSDAY

Fly to Adelaide

FRIDAY

Tour new offices

2 Grammar

Use Paul's diary and write sentences about his week like this:

1 He's attending a computer course on Monday.

2 ....

3 ....

4 ....

5 ....

6 ....

3 Language in use

Before Paul goes to Melbourne, he has to meet his colleague Sandra to discuss the budget for the plant. Put the sentences below in the correct order to form their conversation. Begin like this:

a ☐1 Good morning, Paul speaking.

b ☐ Well, are you free on Wednesday?

c ☐ Bye.

d ☐ I'm seeing Helen at 10, and I'm having lunch with the Sales Manager. How about 4?

e ☐ Hello Paul, this is Sandra. Before you go to Melbourne, I just want to go over the budget with you.

f ☐ Tuesday would be fine. What time?

g ☐ Fine. When would suit you?

h ☐ I'm sorry, I can't manage Wednesday. I'm interviewing all day. How about Tuesday?

i ☐ OK. Tuesday afternoon at 4. That's fine. I'll see you then.

9 Products and services

9.1 Services

1 Vocabulary

What can you use a bank for? Use the following words and phrases to complete the paragraph below.

| withdraw cash | borrow money | pay bills |
| deposit cheques | order ( ) traveller's cheques | |

In everyday life, most people use their bank simply to .... (1) and .... (2). At many banks you can also .... (3). If you want a new car, you might .... (4) from the bank, and if you are going on holiday, you should .... your .... (5) at least a week in advance.

2 Language in use

Put the following conversation between a customer service representative at First Direct and a customer in the correct order.

- [ ] Of course. Which currencies are you interested in?

- [ ] Thank you for calling.

- [ ] US dollars and Japanese Yen.

- [ ] Today's rate is US$1.64 to the pound. For the Yen it's 210.65 to the pound. Is there anything else I can help you with?

- [ ] Hello, First Direct, how can I help you?

- [ ] No, that's all. Thank you for your help.

- [ ] I'd like to find out some prices for foreign currency.

Now listen to the conversation and check your answers.

3 Writing

A friend of yours is thinking of opening a bank account. Write a short note explaining some of the advantages of opening an account with First Direct. You can look at the article about First Direct in your Learner's Book for ideas.

....

....

....

....

....

....

....

....

9.2 Describing a product

1 🔈 ◎ Listening

Listen to these sentences and circle the numbers you hear.

1 60 cm   160 cm
2 44 × 40 × 19 cm   84 × 40 × 90 cm
3 18   8
4 $349 $394
5 $16.90 $6.90
6 1976-32   1967-23

2 Language in use

Write the questions for these answers.

1 How big is it?

   117 × 95.5 × 95.5 cm.

2 ....

   It's got three shelves.

3 ....

   It's made of natural pine.

4 ....

   40 kg.

5 ....

   It costs $298.

6 ....

   Yes, that includes delivery.

3 Reading

Read this advertisement and complete it with words and phrases from the box.

> **a** outstanding feature **b** rigid frame
> **c** solidly constructed **d** pockets
> **e** it won't fall over when you pull it
> **f** through crowded spaces

The carry-on garment bag you don't have to carry

First of all, it's a garment bag that not only hangs and fits into overhead compartments, but rolls .... (1) on two wheels that glide easily over carpet, hard flooring and tarmac. The pulling handle is on the side of the bag so .... (2).

It's .... (3) of a strong, light material. The genuine leather handle is both long-lasting and attractive. Its .... (4) accommodates more clothing with less wrinkling, and also makes the bag stand upright when you set it down, instead of sagging like many hanging bags. It has .... (5) for shoes and shirts and a wide zippered compartment to hold your passport, tickets and luggage straps.

Its most .... (6) is that a bag that makes travelling so much easier is yours for the low price of $89.

9.3 Keeping the customer happy

1 📼 ◎ **Listening**

Listen to the owner of Foodliner, a supermarket, talking about customer service. Choose the correct answer.

1 Foodliner is

  a part of a large supermarket chain.
  b a small family-owned store.
  c a small supermarket.

2 The average waiting time at the checkout is

  a five minutes.   b three minutes.
  c seven minutes.

3 Foodliner runs a bus service for customers

  a every day.   b once a month.
  c once a week.

4 Staff help disabled customers

  a with their shopping.
  b take their shopping home.
  c decide what to buy.

5 Foodliner hopes to

  a reach new customers.
  b satisfy existing customers.
  c expand its store.

2 **Language in use**

You work at Foodliner. You recently received the following letter of complaint. Read the letter, and complete the sentences below.

Dear Sir/Madam

I have been shopping in your store for several years and have always found the staff very helpful.

However, when I was in last week there were several problems. First of all, the brand of soap I usually buy was not available, and no one could tell me when it would be back in stock. Then I had to wait ten minutes to pay for my shopping. Finally, your bus, which picks me up and takes me home again as I do not have a car, had already left!

I would like to hear what you have to say about the problems I had last week. If this happens again, I will be forced to shop somewhere else.

Yours sincerely

Mr G. Beasley

1 Mr Beasley is ....

2 He couldn't find ....

3 He had to wait ....

4 He missed ....

5 He will shop ....

3 **Writing**

Now write a letter to Mr Beasley, apologizing for the problems and offering to help.

Progress test 2

10.1 Grammar

<u>Underline</u> the correct tense in *italics*.

Easy**air** *started / has started* [1] service in 1993. It *flew / has flown* [2] to five destinations and *used / has used* [3] two second-hand aircraft. Since then it *grew / has grown* [4] to a medium sized airline and *carried / has carried* [5] nearly a million passengers. Last year, it *served / has served* [6] 22 destinations. In May it *took / has taken* [7] delivery of seven new aircraft. The number of passengers *grew / has grown* [8] too, with most flights full.

10.2 Language in use

Rewrite each of these sentences another way.

1 Transporting goods by sea is slower than by air.

2 Travelling by train is more environmentally friendly than by air.

3 Sending perishable goods by air is better than by rail.

10.3 Language in use

Write what you would say in these situations:

1 ask for a copy of a company's brochure

2 apologize in advance for missing a meeting

3 confirm a meeting next week

4 thank someone for dinner last week

5 accept an invitation to a conference

6 arrange a meeting for next Thursday

10.4 Vocabulary

Use the words in the box to complete the paragraph below.

| textile   automobiles   coffee   service |
| tourism   petroleum   consumer electronics |
| agricultural   banking   cotton |

Commodities play an important role in many industries. For example, the .... [1] industry relies on .... [2] and wool. The .... [3] industry relies on oil. Rice and .... [4] are important for the .... [5] industry.

   Now let's look at manufacturing and service industries. Manufacturing includes industries such as .... [6] and .... [7]. Today, the .... [8] industries such as advertising, ... [9] and .... [10] play an increasingly important role in many economies. In fact, in many economies these industries are the most important.

10.5 Language in use

Use these prompts to write a short dialogue. Use the correct tense of the verb.

1 fly / Kuala Lumpur / Thursday. Please / book / room / hotel

A: ....

2 OK, I / book / hotel

B: ....

3 I / stay / four nights. Then / I / go / Singapore. Please / send / fax / office / there

A: ....

4 Fine. I / send / fax / Singapore office

B: ....

5 I / meet / Mr Bandur there. Please / send / report / him

A: ....

6 Yes, I / send / report / him

B: ....

10.6 Language in use

Here are some of China's exports. Write sentences using *some*, *a lot of*, etc.

Machinery

Chemicals

Vehicles

Oil

1 China exports ....

....

2 ....

....

3 ....

....

4 ....

....

10.7 Listening

Listen to the message and complete this form.

Name: ....

Company: ....

Model	Units
....	....
....	....
....	....
....	....

Send by (tick): Sea ☐   Air ☐

11 Marketing

11.1 Projecting an image

1 Reading

Read this text about Samsung's new logo and answer these questions.

Samsung gets the blues

SAMSUNG, the South Korean group of companies covering everything from electronics and engineering to finance and insurance, has recently launched a new logo. The corporate logo shows the company's wish to become a world leader in several ways.

The use of the colour blue suggests stability and reliability, and projects a warm and intimate feeling.

The name is now written in English, making it easier to read. It also makes it easier for people all over the world to remember the name.

The shape of the logo symbolizes the world moving through space and gives the image of innovation and change. The first letter 'S' and the last letter 'G' break out of the oval to connect the inside with the outside. This shows Samsung's desire to be one with the world and to serve society as a whole.

1 What colour is the new logo?
2 What does this colour suggest?
3 Why is the name now written in English?
4 What does the shape of the logo symbolize?
5 What is the importance of the first and last letters connecting the interior with the exterior?

2 Listening

Look up any new words below in a dictionary. Then listen to a salesperson talking about the psychology of colours. Match the colours in column A to the qualities in column B.

A	B
1 blue	a cheerfulness
2 green	b confidence and harmony
3 yellow	c tradition and staleness
4 red	d life and growth
5 grey	e age, wisdom and judgement
6 purple	f activity and excitement

3 Language in use

Match a phrase in column A to a phrase in column B like this:

A	B
1 I give my business card to	a which they post or fax to us.
2 Suppliers receive an order form	b new business contacts I meet.
3 We send our catalogue to people	c which contains information about new products.
4 Regular customers receive a newsletter	d who place large orders.
5 We present calendars to customers	e who enquire about our products.

1 Reading

Read this article about sampling and put these headings in the correct place.

> **a** Sampling and advertising
> **b** The growth of sampling
> **c** Does it help sell products?
> **d** Why consumers like it

(1)

Sampling, or giving people small packs of a product to try, is becoming big business. About 250 million samples were distributed to households last year. It's not a new technique. In 1954, Circular Distributors was the first company to use sampling in Britain. It delivered four million bars of Sunlight soap in the north of England and shortly afterwards distributed 10 million retail packs of Omo, a washing powder.

(2)

The attractions of sampling are clear. Consumers are more likely to try a new product if they are given a free sample than if they have to pay the full price for something they may not like.

(3)

But how many people purchase a product after taking advantage of a free sample? Two-thirds of consumers buy a product after receiving a free sample through the door, but only one-third will buy a product they have seen in television ads.

(4)

However, samples are of limited appeal if the public is not aware of the product beforehand. So manufacturers should back up sampling with advertising.

2 Language in use

Write the questions for the answers below.

1 ....

One-third.

2 ....

Sunlight soap.

3 ....

250 million.

4 ....

1954.

3 Vocabulary

Use these clues to complete the word grid.

1 / 3 To increase sales, stores put goods on ... . (2 words)
2 / 4 Selling products by sending information through the post. (2 words)
5 Person who buys goods.
6 Letting people know about products or services.
7 A popular giveaway.
8 Sampling is a form of sales ... .

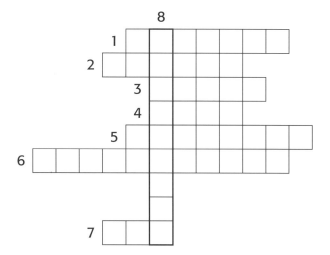

11.3 Choosing a promotional product for your company

1 ▭ ◎ Listening

Listen to the conversation and complete the order form.

promotions plus

ORDER FORM

COMPANY: .... *Moda* ....

CUSTOMER NUMBER: .... (1)

Catalogue number	Quantity	Item	Colour	Price
.... (2)	600	Ballpoint pens	...... (3)	.... (4)
.... (5)	.... (6)	Baseball caps	white	.... (7)

Special instructions:

.... (8)

2 Language in use

Look at this letter from Promotions Plus to Moda. Put the sentences together and in the correct order.

promotions plus
unit 15
bedford industrial estate
stevenage
herts SG11 1PN

moda sportswear
34 rose street
edinburgh EH1 1HZ

dear renzo
1 we look forward to hearing
2 thank you for your recent order
3 and to doing
4 we are pleased to confirm your order for ballpoint pens and
5 for merchandising items
6 that the goods have arrived safely
7 business with you in future
8 baseball caps printed with your company name

yours sincerely

promotions plus

3 Writing

Now rewrite the letter using the correct layout and punctuation.

12 Statistics

12.1 Describing performance

① Vocabulary

Write the expressions in the box under the graphs below.

> a slight increase   a sudden collapse
> a dramatic rise   a steady decline
> a gradual rise   a jump

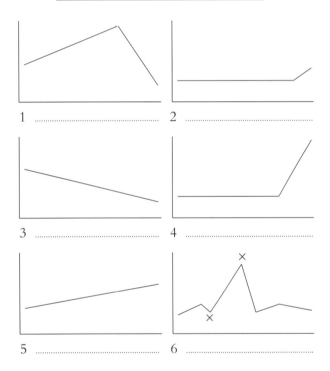

1 ....   2 ....

3 ....   4 ....

5 ....   6 ....

② Grammar

Underline the correct word in *italics*.

Demand for copper declined *gradual / gradually* [1] over a period of five years. At the same time there was a *sharp / sharply* [2] increase in competition among producers. This caused a *slight / slightly* [3] fall in prices throughout world markets. The market grew *slow / slowly* [4] during the years that followed. Competition, however, increased *strong / strongly* [5], and this kept prices very low.

③ Language in use

Look at the chart showing a company's results from 1993 to 1998 and use the verbs and phrases in the box to complete the paragraph below.

> plunge   remain stable
> climb   decline   soar

The company made good profits of £20 million in 1993. With the introduction of new equipment and an improvement in the economy, profits .... [1] in 1994 to £95 million. Sales continued strong, and profits for 1995 .... [2] to £105 million. In 1996, the company suffered serious problems and profits .... [3] to £45 million. In 1997 they .... [4] a little further to £40 million and .... [5] in 1998 at £40 million.

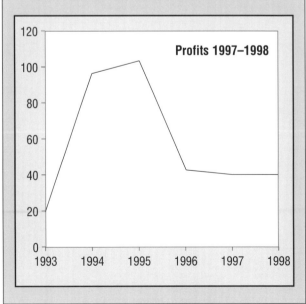

Profits 1997–1998

12.2 Cause and effect

1 Reading

Read this passage about Hyundai car sales and complete the key for the graph below.

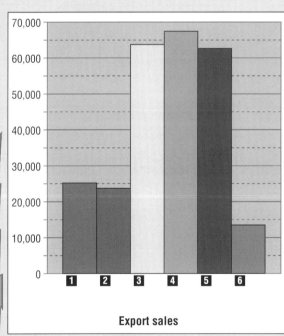

 Hyundai had a very successful year for export sales, with sales up strongly in every region except Latin America, which suffered a very small decline. Overall, exports increased by 27 per cent over the previous year. Starting with our biggest export region, not including the European Union and North America, sales in the Pacific region reached 67,431 vehicles this year. This was followed by China, with 63,915 and Latin America with 62,760. Sales in Eastern Europe grew by an astonishing 66.7 per cent to a total of 25,265 vehicles. Sales of 24,086 vehicles were achieved in Africa, and 13,729 in the rest of Asia excluding Korea and China. Altogether, Hyundai sold 494,626 vehicles in export sales. Hyundai is now building new factories overseas to meet the world-wide demand for its vehicles.

Export sales

Key

1 .... 4 ....

2 .... 5 ....

3 .... 6 ....

2 Writing

Match the two halves of the sentences below. Then rewrite them using *because of / due to / as a result of.*

1 The new Elantra model was successful ...

2 Overall sales grew ...

3 African sales should rise ...

4 By 2000, Hyundai's overseas production will reach 500,000 vehicles a year ...

... Hyundai exporting to new markets.

... new plants being built in Egypt, Botswana and Zimbabwe.

... Hyundai's good reputation.

... world-wide demand for its vehicles.

1 ....

2 ....

3 ....

4 ....

3 Listening

Listen to the following report and choose the correct answer.

1 How much did Hyundai invest in its new plant in India?
   a US$70 million   b US$700 million
   c US$7,000 million

2 How many cars will the new factory in India produce every year?
   a 10,000   b 1,000,000   c 100,000

3 Who will buy the cars produced at this factory?
   a families who need a small car
   b people who cannot afford a bigger car
   c young people

4 In the second stage, how many cars will Hyundai be able to produce?
   a 200,000   b 20,000   c 2,000,000

5 In which country does Hyundai not have plans for a factory?
   a Venezuela   b Brazil   c Turkey

12.3 Presenting information

1 Reading

These sentences are missing from this text about giving presentations. Where do they belong?

a Make sure that your presentation has a clear theme.
b Good presentations are always the result of good planning.
c Who is the audience for your presentation?
d Most people become nervous when thinking about a presentation.

Giving a presentation

.... (1) The challenges are to catch and keep the attention of the audience, to perform well throughout without 'drying up', to avoid speaking too quickly or giving nervous body language and to give a clear account of what you want to say.

.... (2) You must have a clear idea of why you are giving the presentation. Consider what you want your audience to do as a result of your presentation.

.... (3) You will need to know how many people will be at the presentation. You should also know how knowledgeable they are about the subject of your presentation.

.... (4) You should start by stating what the purpose of the presentation is, what structure you will follow and perhaps how long it will be. You should finish with a conclusion which summarizes the important points and a recommendation, suggestion or request for the audience to act in a certain way.

2 Language in use

Put these phrases for structuring a presentation in the right order.

a ☐ Let's start by looking at last year's sales figures.

b ☐ Welcome to the annual sales conference.

c ☐ If we move on to our plans for next year, you'll see the changes we want to make.

d ☐ To finish, I'd like to wish you all a successful year.

e ☐ I'm going to talk about our sales last year and our plans for the coming year.

3 ▭ ◉ Listening

Part 1

Listen to Peter Gammer talking about a presentation he gave some years ago. Are these statements true (T) or false (F)?

1 The presentation was to be 90 minutes. ☐

2 The first quarter of an hour went well. ☐

3 He stopped the presentation after 45 minutes. ☐

Part 2

Now listen to him talking about the lessons he learned. Tick all the things he says you should do to give a successful presentation.

a Tell the audience jokes. ☐

b Think about what the audience wants to hear. ☐

c Tell the audience what is of interest to you. ☐

d Have more material than you will need. ☐

e Spend 60 minutes preparing for every 5 minutes of your presentation. ☐

f Practise your presentation several times. ☐

13 Money

13.1 Negotiating the price

1 Reading

Read this article and tick (✔) the points the writer makes.

1 Red pens can lose you a sale. ☐

2 It is impossible to make a sale in bad weather. ☐

3 Customers like to feel they are being told a secret. ☐

4 Arguing with customers makes them respect you. ☐

5 Try to establish something in common with a customer. ☐

How to get that sale

If it's raining or snowing, you will usually sell. Most people think you need good weather to make a sale. But on a bad day, your customers will not have as many distractions.

Don't ever offer a red pen or pencil to a customer to sign the agreement. This makes them think 'Stop'. Don't wear any red clothing. If possible, use blues and greens.

Do or say something your customer can relate to. For example, if your customer drives a truck, so does your father. This establishes common ground.

Always tell the customer a secret. Customers love to think they know something special.

Never argue with the customer. You can win the argument, but you will lose the sale.

2 Language in use

Complete the dialogue with expressions from the box.

> **a** you take the demonstration model
> **b** if I pay cash   **c** that's rather high
> **d** I'm afraid that's not possible

CUSTOMER: So how much does this van cost?

SALESPERSON: $36,000.

CUSTOMER: .... (1).
              Will you give me a discount
              .... (2)?

SALESPERSON: What kind of discount did you have in mind?

CUSTOMER: 10 per cent.

SALESPERSON: .... (3). But if
              .... (4), we might
              be able to reach an agreement.

3 Writing

Complete these sentences about yourself.

1 If it rains tomorrow,

....

2 If the weather's good tomorrow,

....

3 I'll go swimming tomorrow, if

....

4 I'll take a holiday in July, if

....

5 I won't be able to buy a new car, if

....

6 If I buy a new computer,

....

35

Listening

Money we owe · Money owed to us

Part 1

Listen to Inez Murphy, a businesswoman, talking about slow payers. Then write answers to these questions.

1 Why can't her customers pay?

....

2 What kind of discount is she offering for prompt payment?

....

3 How long can her business survive like this?

....

Part 2

Now listen to a businessman talking about his company's credit control system and write answers to these questions.

4 How many days is the agreement on invoices?

....

5 How long does it now take customers to pay?

....

6 How much does this cost the company a year?

....

② Writing

Use these prompts to make sentences giving advice on controlling credit.

1 customer / bad credit record / (not) give / them / credit

If ....

2 someone promises payment / it doesn't come / chase immediately

....

3 ask a debt collector / help / customer / refuses / pay

....

4 you want prompt payment / make sure / invoices correct

....

③ Vocabulary

Use the words in the box to complete the paragraph below.

| reminders | credit | chasing |
| invoices | collect | overdue |

Cash flow is a serious problem for many small businesses. .... (1) can remain unpaid for several months, and these .... (2) accounts cost businesses money. You can send .... (3) letters and other .... (4), but even these sometimes do not work. These small businesses will themselves need .... (5) so that they have money to pay their bills. In this way, the problem spreads to others, who will in turn have to .... (6) money from the small businesses.

13.3 Chasing payment

① Vocabulary

Who usually does what? Write C (Customer) or S (Supplier) like this:

a [C] Places an order

b [ ] Issues an invoice

c [ ] Sends a reminder

d [ ] Confirms the order

e [ ] Dispatches the goods

f [ ] Settles the invoice

Now put them in the order in which they happen:

1 *a* → 2 .... → 3 .... →

4 .... → 5 .... → 6 ....

② 🔊 Listening

Listen to these voice mail messages and complete the message pads.

1
From:
Company: HyperTech
Invoice number:
Message:

2
From: Arnold Simms
Company: WordText
Invoice number:
Message:

③ Language in use

Match the sentences in column A with the sentences in column B like this:

A

1 We haven't received all the goods we ordered.

2 We've lost your invoice.

3 The invoice must have gone to the wrong department.

4 Some of the goods were faulty.

5 We ordered 800, but your invoice was for 1,800.

6 Our cheque is in the post.

B

a Please send a new one clearly marked 'Purchasing Department'.

b Please send us a correct invoice.

c We'll send you a cheque as soon as they arrive.

d Please send us a receipt as soon as you receive it.

e We will not pay until they are replaced.

f Please send us a copy.

14 Socializing

14.1 Gift-giving

1 🔲 ◎ Listening

Listen to a woman talking about gift-giving in the United States. Tick (✔) the correct statements.

1 Americans always remember special occasions on the day. ☐

2 They open the gift in front of others. ☐

3 They always write a thank-you note after receiving a gift. ☐

4 If you go to someone's house, you should take flowers and a small gift. ☐

2 Reading

Read this article and choose the correct answer.

1 For European business, the Christmas season starts in

   a September.   b November.
   c December.

2 Swiss business people

   a do not give many presents.
   b receive presents from the bankers.
   c often give presents to their bankers.

3 Italian business people give presents to

   a all their customers.   b charities.
   c nobody.

4 In the UK, most companies send

   a 50,000 Christmas cards.
   b cards with a Christmas theme.
   c about 400 Christmas cards.

Christmas giving

Christmas comes but once a year – and lasts about four months as far as European business is concerned. Planning for the seasonal strategy begins in the summer, with the advertising campaigns ready to roll in early autumn. In the UK some companies even start planning their Christmas gift-giving as early as mid-summer.

In general, however, continental European companies are more generous gift-givers. The Swiss are particularly keen to appear bountiful. Some bankers routinely receive gifts – porcelain, Art Deco work, silver – worth up to £700 each! In Italy it is polite to give presents to almost everyone you deal with, including, for example, your doctor. Business associates once benefited too, until scandals and the recession stopped corporate generosity. Companies still want to appear to be generous, so donations are given – with much publicity – to charities.

While the UK may be some way below continental Europe in gift-giving, it does take its Christmas cards very seriously. According to a London-based card maker, UK companies send an average of 400 Christmas cards each. Some send as many as 50,000. Less than 1% of firms send cards depicting Christmas scenes.

3 Writing

You are about to leave on a business trip. What gift would you take for your hosts? Write a short paragraph describing it and why it is suitable.

14.2 Planning a free day

1 Reading

Read this article and answer the following questions.

1 According to the article, do businessmen enjoy trips?
2 What are some of the problems of businesswomen travelling alone?
3 Who set up Global Network?
4 Who can become a member of Global Network?
5 What services does Global Network provide?

Businesswomen on the road

Lonely and boring. That's how many businessmen describe their business trips. Add to that worries about safety when travelling alone and finding your room equipped with a trouser press but no skirt hangers and you have a typical businesswoman's travel experience.

Many hotels are trying to be more female-friendly and now train staff not to make women dining alone feel unwanted. They also provide secure parking and other services to help women feel safer.

But you could be staying at the friendliest, most security-conscious hotel in the world and still be bored. 'I found eating on my own in the evening really miserable. Then after the meal what do you do? You don't feel comfortable in the bar, so it's room service, TV, papers or a book – it gets really boring,' explains Diane Newhofer, who travelled for 20 years.

She founded Global Network to help solve these problems. This puts professional women who will be in the same place at the same time in touch, and provides members with information about user-friendly hotels, gyms and restaurants for women travelling alone. Ann Seligman, a shipping manager for an international timber firm, has found the service invaluable. 'I'm a confident person, but I hate eating alone, especially if they put you in the back or in the corner. Meeting a colleague through Global Network is a great advantage.'

2 Grammar

Make these questions more polite like this:

1 What time is breakfast?
   Could you tell me what time breakfast is?

2 Where can I change money?
   ....

3 What time does the bank open?
   ....

4 Where is the business centre?
   ....

5 What number bus do I need to get to the exhibition centre?
   ....

6 How often does the bus to the exhibition centre run?
   ....

3 Language in use

Put the following sentences in the correct order to form a conversation.

a ☐ Yes, I'd like some information about what's on in Buenos Aires this week.

b ☐ Yes, there's a branch of American Express just a few blocks away in San Martin Square.

c ☐ Of course. We have this leaflet, which lists everything that's on this week.

d ☐ Thank you. Oh, could you tell me where I can cash a traveller's cheque?

e ☐ Hello, can I help you?

f ☐ Goodbye.

g ☐ Thanks very much, goodbye.

14.3 Eating out

1 Listening

Part 1

Listen to a woman talking about business entertaining in the United States and tick (✔) the correct statements.

1 Business dinners are popular in the United States. ☐

2 Breakfast is a popular time to do business. ☐

3 Lunches usually last for two hours. ☐

4 You must never socialize at a business lunch. ☐

Part 2

Now listen to a man talking about business entertaining in Korea and tick (✔) the correct statements.

5 Koreans prefer business lunches to business dinners. ☐

6 Business dinners usually involve a lot of drinking. ☐

7 The dinners finish quite early. ☐

8 The aim of the business dinner is to get to know each other. ☐

2 Language in use

Match a question on the left with a reply on the right.

1 Would you like a starter?

2 What would you like to drink?

3 What will you have as a main course?

4 Would you like boiled or roast potatoes?

5 Would you like a dessert?

a I think I'll have the fish.

b Mineral water, please.

c No, thank you. Just coffee, please.

d Yes, some soup would be nice.

e Roast, please.

3 Vocabulary

Use these clues to complete the word grid.

1 Often served as a starter.
2 To cook in an oven at a high temperature.
3 Hot drink served at the end of a meal.
4 Made of green, leafy vegetables and tossed with oil and vinegar.
5 A root vegetable that can be boiled, fried or roasted.

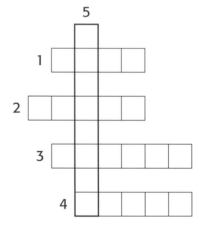

Progress test 3

15.1 Vocabulary

Use the verbs in the box in the correct tense to complete these paragraphs.

rise	fall	soar	increase	climb	plunge	decrease

Sales for Company 1 .... (1)
from 280,000 in 1993 to 110,000 in 1994. They
then .... (2) slightly in 1995 and
1996 to 100,000, and finally in 1997 they

.... (3) to 180,000.

Sales for Company 2 .... (4)
from 50,000 in 1993 to 200,000 in 1994. They
.... (5) further to 220,000 in 1995,
but .... (6) to 180,000 in 1996.
They .... (7) to 210,000 in 1997.

15.2 Language in use

Rewrite these questions in a more polite form.

1 Where is the train station?

....

2 What time does the bus leave?

....

3 When do the shops close today?

....

Rewrite these questions in a simpler form.

4 Could you tell me how I get to the conference centre?

....

5 Do you know when breakfast is served?

....

6 Could you tell me the restaurant's phone number?

....

15.3 Grammar

<u>Underline</u> **the correct form of the words in** *italics*.

Prices rose *sharp / sharply* (1) four years ago, and in the following two years there was a *steady / steadily* (2) climb. Last year there was a *sharp / sharply* (3) decline, and this year they fell *dramatic / dramatically* (4). Forecasts for next year suggest that prices will climb *steady / steadily* (5), but after that there will be a *slow / slowly* (6) fall.

15.4 Grammar

Join these prompts with *who* or *which* and make complete sentences.

1 Credit Controller / someone / check / invoices / paid

....

....

2 First Direct / bank / have / no branches

....

....

3 Oil / product / Mexico / export

....

....

4 Computers / machines / help / businesses

....

....

5 a programmer / someone / write / computer programs

....

....

15.5 Vocabulary

Put the words in the box under the appropriate headings.

> salad fry beef beans grill Brussels sprouts
> roast spinach lamb potatoes pork
> chicken boil ham steam

Cooking methods	Meats	Vegetables
....	....	....
....	....	....
....	....	....
....	....	....
....	....	....

15.6 Grammar

Use these prompts to make *if + will* sentences.

1 sales / (not) improve / (not) make / profit

....

....

2 profits high / we / get / pay increase

....

....

3 I / lower price / you / pay / cash

....

....

4 you / take 10,000 / we / give / you / discount

....

....

5 we / give / you / 60 days' credit / you / pay / delivery

....

....

15.7 🔊 Listening

Listen to this interview and choose the correct answers. In some cases there is more than one correct answer.

1 The company decided to change their logo because

a they were tired of the old look.
b they had been receiving bad publicity.
c they had a new product.

2 The company want its new logo to appear

a fresh and colourful.
b stable and unchanging.
c serious and modern.

3 The new logo

a is a different colour from the old.
b shows all the kinds of businesses they are in.
c involved a lot of decision making.

4 The change of logo has

a been too difficult.
b improved the company's image.
c brought good publicity.

16 Business culture and ethics

16.1 Corporate culture

1 Reading

Read this article about European management styles. In which country:

1 are managers specialists in their field?
2 are managers experts in several fields?
3 are managers good at mixing with different people?
4 are contacts important?
5 do managers have experience of all departments?

A question of culture

Bosses in France are like their famous general, Napoleon – they are brilliant planners who are experts in industry, finance and government. Their companies have a strict management structure which divides bosses and their workers.

Managers in Italy are more flexible. Rules and regulations matter less than friends and family contacts. What goes on in a meeting is often less important than what happens before and after. This can shock Germans, who like to do everything according to the rules. Board members have years of technical training and a German manager will not move out of their special field before reaching board level. This is in contrast to Britain, where tomorrow's managers are sent through every department in the firm to give them a broad, but not always thorough, overview of its operations.

To avoid clashes between these national cultures, some European companies prefer Swedish or Swiss chief executives, who are better at dealing with all kinds of people.

2 Vocabulary

Complete these sentences. Then write the missing words in the puzzle below.

1 A .... is a large building used to store goods.

2 In factories, workers wear .... to protect their clothes.

3 Anyone can do this job, no .... experience necessary.

4 A busy .... might have to attend several meetings a day and travel a lot.

5 People who work for a company are called its ....

6 .... are responsible for running a company and making business decisions.

3 Writing

Look at the texts on page 89 in your Learner's Book again. Write sentences saying which company is most like yours and why or which company you would prefer to work for and why.

16.2 Everyday dilemmas

❶ Vocabulary

Match a word in column A to a word in column B like this:

A	B
office	account
computer	supplies
personal	report
confidential	software
expense	calls

(arrow drawn from "office" to "supplies")

Now use the words you have matched in the following sentences.

1 Although it is illegal, many people copy

....

for use on their home computers.

2 Adding extra items to your ....

.... or making a lot of

....

at work are two examples of wasting your company's money.

3 If someone gave you a ....

...................., would you look

at it?

4 Some people at work take paper and other

....

home with them.

❷ 📼 ◉ Listening

Listen to two people talking about problems they have in the office. Are these statements true (T) or false (F)?

1 Customers can make free calls on the 800 number. ☐

2 One employee makes personal calls to her family on the 800 number. ☐

3 Her family live locally. ☐

4 The department head took her department out to lunch. ☐

5 The staff paid $10 each towards the bill. ☐

6 The woman put the bill on her expense account. ☐

❸ Reading

Read this letter and choose the best answer to the questions below.

I am a sales professional for a software company. My boss, the Sales Manager, doesn't always tell the truth. Sometimes he makes our products sound better than they are – which I think is bad for business – or he says he has finished a task when he has not.

The real problem began at a departmental meeting with the CEO last month. My manager said he had sent a new marketing strategy out to his staff. I know he hasn't even begun to work on it. The CEO was angry that my colleagues and I had not started using these new instructions – but we haven't even received them! It is hard to complain, because the CEO and the Sales Manager are good friends. Nobody in our department is very happy about the situation. What should I do?

1 The writer has a problem with

　a her colleagues.　b the CEO.
　c her boss.

2 The Sales Manager tells customers

　a bad things about the products.
　b bad things about other products.
　c that their products are better than they really are.

3 The Sales Manager

　a hasn't begun work on the new marketing plan.
　b has completed the plan but not sent it to the sales staff.
　c has circulated the plan to all staff.

16.3 A woman's place

1 🔊 Listening

A woman is talking about women in work in the year 2010. Decide what the words in the blanks are. Then listen and compare your answers.

By the year 2010, I .... (1) that the situation of women in work will have changed dramatically. Already in Britain there are a growing number of women doctors and lawyers, and I'm .... (2) that growth in these fields will continue. Women have traditionally been confined to clerical jobs – 'women's work' such as secretarial jobs. But this is changing. It's .... (3) that we will see more men doing these jobs in future as women move into managerial and executive positions. It's .... (4) that by 2010 there will be any idea of men's or women's jobs, whoever is best at a job will be the one who gets it. And I'm .... (5) that this means a big change in the job market for women.

2 Language in use

Match the two halves of the sentences below.

1 It's likely
2 I'm certain
3 Perhaps
4 It's unlikely
5 She's certain

a that she'll get a promotion at work.

b that computers will be essential to daily life by 1999.

c I'll go to Spain next year, I don't know.

d that I'll live to see the year 2050!

e that economic problems will be solved by 2020.

1 ....

2 ....

3 ....

4 ....

5 ....

3 Writing

Think ahead to the year 2020. Write five predictions about what life will be like then.

1 ....

2 ....

3 ....

4 ....

5 ....

17 Meetings

17.1 Greening the office

1 🔈 ◉ Listening

Listen to a representative from Stena Line explaining how the company has become more environmentally friendly, and tick (✔) the correct statements.

1 Stena Line now uses fuel with a higher sulphur content. ☐

2 Stena Line is cooperating with other organizations to improve the environment. ☐

3 Tanks on board the ships purify waste water. ☐

4 Stena separates glass and aluminium for recycling. ☐

5 Environmentally friendly products have replaced disposable ones. ☐

6 90 per cent of all cleaning fluids used on the ships are environmentally friendly. ☐

2 Language in use

Write a dialogue based on the prompts like this:

A: (Suggest using recycled paper. Ask for an opinion.)

I suggest using recycled paper. What do you think?

B: (Agree.)

....

....

A: (Suggest that people travel to work by bus. Ask for an opinion.)

....

....

B: (Disagree. Give a reason.)

....

....

3 Writing

Write some suggestions for ways you could be more green at home or work.

....

....

....

....

....

17.2 Reporting

1 Grammar

Tick (✔) the correct sentence in each pair.

1 a She said they should try to reuse waste paper. ✔

  b She said him they should try to reuse waste paper. ☐

2 a He suggested to use proper plates instead of paper ones. ☐

  b He suggested using proper plates instead of paper ones. ☐

3 a She told that they had no place to wash dishes. ☐

  b She told him that they had no place to wash dishes. ☐

4 a She also pointed out that washing plates would mean more space and labour. ☐

  b She also pointed out to wash plates would mean more space and labour. ☐

5 a He recommended to reduce packaging. ☐

  b He recommended reducing packaging. ☐

6 a She agreed to find ways of doing this. ☐

  b She agreed finding ways of doing this. ☐

2 ▭ ◎ Listening

Listen to an extract from a meeting and choose the correct answer.

1 Laura found out that their present supplier

  a can supply glass bottles.
  b only supplies plastic bottles.
  c refused to supply glass bottles.

2 The glass bottles are

  a the same price as plastic bottles.
  b cheaper than plastic bottles.
  c slightly more expensive than plastic bottles.

3 Laura thinks they should

  a get a new supplier.
  b stay with the present supplier.
  c find a more helpful supplier.

4 James

  a thinks plastic is more convenient.
  b wants to use glass bottles.
  c doesn't like plastic bottles.

5 Max feels that

  a plastic is better for recycling.
  b it will not be possible to use glass.
  c glass will be better for the image of the new bath oil.

3 Writing

Look at these sentences from the tapescript. Rewrite them as reported speech.

1 CHAIR: Laura, can you tell us what you found out about glass bottles?

The Chair asked Laura to tell them
what she found out about glass
bottles.

2 LAURA: I contacted several other suppliers, and the prices are pretty much the same.

3 JAMES: I really think that using glass is a mistake.

4 MAX: James, convenience isn't everything!

5 LAURA: I suggest using glass bottles as the price is going to be nearly the same.

17.3 Cutting costs

1 Language in use

Match these expressions in column A with their functions in column B like this:

A

1 Let's not get sidetracked.
2 Let's start.
3 Can I just say something?
4 Can I just finish?
5 Sorry to interrupt, but ...

B

a starting
b interrupting
c dealing with interruptions
d keeping to the point
e interrupting

2 ▭ ◎ Listening

Listen to an extract from a meeting. You will hear four beeps. Listen again, and for each beep, decide which of the expressions 1 to 5 in column A above would be suitable.

Beep 1 ☐   Beep 2 ☐
Beep 3 ☐   Beep 4 ☐

3 Writing

You are chairing this meeting. What would you say?

CHAIR (1):   (start meeting / introduce Paola)

....

....

PAOLA: Thank you. As you know, we want to make the office more environmentally friendly. One suggestion is to use less energy for heating.

RICHARD: Sorry Paola, but it would be cold in here! I can't agree to that!

CHAIR (2):   (deal with the interruption / ask Paola to continue)

....

....

PAOLA: We also need to look at the amount of paper we use.

SYLVIA: Sorry to interrupt, but I haven't had my new business cards.

CHAIR (3):   (keep to the point / ask Paola to continue)

....

....

PAOLA: For example, last year we doubled the amount of paper we used.

RICHARD: Well, our business doubled last year too.

CHAIR (4):   (move to next point)

....

....

PAOLA: My next point is the use of cars. Too many people drive to work, when there is a good bus service to the office.

SYLVIA: It isn't very good from where I live! There's only one bus an hour –

CHAIR (5):   (keep to the point / any other points?)

....

....

PAOLA: Those are the main points for discussion. Shall we start with the heating, where costs rose ...

18 Processes

18.1 Talking about regulations

❶ Language in use

Here is your contract for your job. Read it and choose the correct verb from the box below to complete the sentences.

> don't have to   can   mustn't   must   cannot

Position: Manager

Your hours of work are 8.30 to 5.00. You

.... (1) be at work during

these hours. If necessary, you

.... (2) come in early or

stay later, but you .... (3)

leave before 5.00. The building is locked

at 7 p.m., so you .... (4)

stay any later than that. This is quite

an informal office, so you

.... (5) wear formal

clothes, although you must be smartly

dressed.

❷ Writing

Complete these sentences using the verbs from exercise 1.

1 I .... work 40 hours a
week.

2 If I do a lot of overtime, I
.... take time off.

3 I .... start work before
7 a.m.

4 I .... work at the
weekend.

5 I .... take my holiday in
the summer.

6 If I am ill, I .... come to
work.

❸ Vocabulary

Use these clues to complete the word grid.

1 Time when you are not at work and can do as you like.
2 Extra hours you have to work.
3 A fixed period of work.
4 Time when you must be at work.
5 You can decide what hours you want to work.

18.2 Describing a process

① 📼 ◎ Listening

Listen to someone from Nike talking about how Nike shoes are made and put these steps in the correct order.

a ☐ Production of the shoes is planned by engineers in both countries.

b ☐ The shoes are produced at contractors' factories around the region.

c ☐ The plans are faxed to manufacturing companies in South Korea.

d ☐ The designs are sent by satellite to Taiwan.

e ☐ Shoes are designed at the company's headquarters in Oregon, USA.

f ☐ The blueprints are developed into prototype shoes.

② Writing

Use these prompts to make sentences to describe a process.

1 coffee beans / collect / farmers

....

2 beans / dry / in the sun

....

3 beans / roast / in ovens

....

4 beans / sort / by workers

....

5 bags / pack / by machine

....

6 bags / transport / to market / by sea

....

③ Reading

Use the words in the box to complete the instructions.

| Then   Finally   First   Next |

.... , open the phone so that you can see the buttons.

.... press the 'Talk' key.

.... , dial the number. If you have programmed certain numbers into the phone, press the 'Memory' key followed by the code for the number you want.

.... , when you have finished, press the 'End' key and close the phone.

18.3 Company history

❶ Reading

Read this article about Volvo cars. Then choose the correct answer to the questions below.

The Essential Volvo

IN 1915 VOLVO was established as the trade name of the Svenska Kullagerfabriken, whose motor car company was formed in 1927.

In the 1920s and 1930s Volvo was not influenced by design outside Sweden. In 1939, however, the PV36 Carioco was launched. This car, named after a Latin American dance, was the first which was American in style.

The decision to use American style paid off in the 1950s, when people in the United States started buying Volvos. The first big-selling model was the PV444 of 1947. Although it was nearly 10 years old when it was launched in the States, it was popular because it was so different from American cars which changed every year.

Volvo launched the Amazon in 1957. It was the first clearly safety-conscious Volvo and the first production car in the world to feature safety belts as standard. Safety features of Volvos became important in marketing.

In the 1960s, the company introduced the P1800 sports car. This was the car used in *The Saint*, the British TV series that proved to be the most effective advertising campaign Volvo ever had. Over 50% of total production of this car was sold in the USA. Today the USA is still Volvo's largest market.

1 What year was Volvo cars created as a company?
a 1915   b 1927   c 1939

2 The PV36 Carioco took its name from
a an American style.   b an American city.
c a Latin American dance.

3 Although it was 10 years old when launched in the USA, the PV444 was popular because
a its design stayed the same.
b its design changed every year.
c it was old.

4 The Amazon was the first production car to
a be safety conscious.
b feature safety belts as standard.
c be marketed as a safe car.

5 The P1800 sports car was successful because
a it featured in a TV series.
b a film star owned one.
c it had an effective advertising campaign.

❷ Grammar

Put the verb in (brackets) into the correct tense to complete these sentences like this:

1 In 1915 the name 'Volvo' *was used* (*use*) ⁽¹⁾ for the first time as a trade name.

2 In 1927 the name .... (*apply*) ⁽²⁾ to a range of cars.

3 Before World War Two, Volvo cars .... (*design*) ⁽³⁾ only for Sweden.

4 The Carioco .... (*name*) ⁽⁴⁾ after a Latin American dance.

5 The PV444 .... (*love*) ⁽⁵⁾ by Americans.

6 The P1800 .... (*advertise*) ⁽⁶⁾ in a TV series.

❸ Grammar

Match the two halves of the sentences like this:

1 Volvo cars	a was launched.
2 In the 1930s Volvo cars	b provided good publicity.
3 In 1939 the Carioco	c became popular in the United States.
4 In the 1950s Volvos	d were not influenced by design outside Sweden.
5 In 1957 Volvo	e produced a car with safety belts as standard.
6 In the 1960s a TV series	f was founded in 1927.

Now listen and check your answers.

19 Conferences

19.1 Finding a location

① 🔊 Listening

You work for Ocean Sound, a computer sound systems company, and are helping to arrange the annual sales conference. Listen to this voice mail message and number these points in the order in which they are mentioned.

a ☐ Think about the conference schedule.

b ☐ Ask participants about problems or preferences.

c ☐ Send out details of when it is taking place so rooms can be booked.

d ☐ Find out about hotels and the best dates for availability.

e ☐ Organize social programme.

② Writing

The conference is to be held in Bangkok at the Central Plaza Hotel. Write a fax to the hotel confirming your booking. Include the following:

- book the large conference room 15–17 June
- book the private dining room 14–17 June – mention the Welcome dinner on 14 June
- book 5 double rooms and 17 singles for the nights of 14–18 June. All 27 participants are arriving the day before the conference starts.

FAX

To: _Central Plaza Hotel, Bangkok_

From: _____

Message

_____

_____

_____

_____

_____

---

③ Writing

Look at the formal invitation to the conference. Correct the capitalization and punctuation.

OCEAN SOUND

dear

i am pleased to invite you to this year's sales conference it will be held at the central plaza hotel bangkok on 15 to 17 june

there will be a welcome dinner on the night of 14 june and your rooms have been reserved for the nights of 14 to 17 june

the central plaza hotel is situated in the heart of bangkok the hotel is organizing a tour of the grand palace on the night of 15 june and on the night of 16 june there will be a dance at the hotel for participants

if there are any problems please write to the conference coordinator, lee bristow

i look forward to seeing you at the conference

1 Reading

This is the programme for the conference. Look at it and read the memo from the Director. Then make the changes to the programme.

June 15	June 16
Director's Welcome and Annual Report	New products 3: KF5000
Coffee	*Coffee*
New products 1: KK90	New marketing strategies 2
Break	*Break*
New products 2: KS300	Question and answer session
Lunch	*Lunch*
New marketing strategies 1	Plans for next year
Tea	*Tea*
Regional reports	Presentation of Sales Awards
Dinner	*Dinner*
Tour of the Grand Palace	*Dance*

MEMO

FROM: The Director
TO: Lee Bristow

I would like to make a few changes to the programme. There are quite a few important sessions that we have to try to fit into the schedule, and I feel that a few sessions are not very important.

First of all, there is no time to present the KL6000, so we need to find a time for that. It is a very important new product. I suggest that we do this after coffee on 16 June. The New marketing strategies 2 session then comes after the break. There will be no question and answer session.

I also think that we need time for a detailed report on this year's sales. The only way I can see to do this is to change the programme for the afternoon of 16 June. The Report on this year's sales will come after lunch, followed by the Plans for next year session. The Sales Awards can be presented at dinner on 15 June.

2 🔲 ◎ Listening

Listen to this voice mail from the Director. Are these statements true (T) or false (F)?

1 The 'Report on this year's sales' is now going to be the last session on 15 June. ☐

2 'Regional reports' is now going to be before lunch on 16 June. ☐

3 The tour has been changed to the evening of 16 June. ☐

4 You must now find a new activity for the evening of 16 June. ☐

19.3 Presenting your product

① Reading

Read the following brochure and answer these questions.

1. What does Ocean Sound produce?
2. What do the sound schemes allow you to do?
3. What are the advantages of the KL6000?
4. Describe one of the new products currently being developed.

OCEAN SOUND

25 years of computer sound effects

We aim to make computing fun by providing sound effects to accompany various actions on the computer. For example, when you open or close a file, the computer makes a sound to let you know what it is doing. These sounds make computing more enjoyable and allow you to personalize your computer. They also help people who have trouble with their sight by providing an audible signal of what the computer has done. The sounds we developed for the Grapheio word processing programs have been highly praised because they make it easier to use the software.

CD players are becoming more common in computers, and our system lets you play music while you work. You can also change the way the music sounds by using our soundByte system.

The new KL6000 is the very latest in home entertainment sound technology. We have already signed contracts for the use of this software in new games being developed for the next generation of computers. The KL6000 offers faster processing and high quality sound reproduction to take you into a total virtual environment. Computer graphics now look almost totally life-like: we aim to make the sound quality match the pictures.

Sound effects for even the smallest hand-held games and software to personalize electronic voices are two new products being developed. The miniature sound effects will open a new world of realism for small computer games, while the improved electronic voices mean that you can create text and then make it sound almost like you!

② Writing

As the conference organizer, you have to write the Director's opening speech. Write a short speech in five paragraphs under the following headings:

Welcome the audience

....
....
....

Introduce yourself (as the Director)

....
....
....

Say what the company does

....
....
....
....

Describe the KL6000

....
....
....
....

Thank the participants for coming to the conference

....
....
....
....

Progress test 4

20.1 Grammar

Fill in the blanks with the correct tense (past simple or present perfect) of the verb in (brackets).

In 1993, the company .... (*make*) [1] a large profit. Since then, profits .... (*fall*) [2] slightly each year. This year, we .... (*lose*) [3] money for the first time in our history. Therefore, we .... (*decide*) [4] to close one factory and reduce the number of workers. After the meeting last week we .... (*say*) [5] that there would be no further job losses. We also .... (*tell*) [6] workers that we need their help to save the company. To thank workers for their help, we .... (*reach*) [7] agreement on conditions.

20.2 Grammar

Write the words these people said.

1 Mary said that she needed a new assistant.

....

2 Lee recommended hiring someone who spoke several languages.

....

3 Sandra asked me to write the advertisement.

....

Write these statements as reported speech.

Gina   Rolando   Maria

4 ....

5 ....

6 ....

20.3 Grammar

You made these notes about new office rules.

1 smoke in the office – forbidden
2 eat lunch anytime between 12 and 2 – allowed
3 finish work at 5 – no rule
4 work 42 hours a week – obligatory
5 make personal calls – forbidden
6 start work at 7.30 – no rule

Now write sentences using the words in the box below.

| have to   don't have to   can |
| can   cannot   must not |

1 ....

2 ....

3 ....

4 ....

5 ....

6 ....

20.4 Grammar

Change these sentences from active to passive voice.

1 Secretaries typed letters.

2 Alan Turing invented the computer.

3 Robots weld the body to the frame.

4 People send orders by E-mail.

Now change these sentences from the passive to the active voice.

5 Cotton is harvested by machines.

6 Cargoes were taken around the world by ship.

7 Cars are assembled by robots.

20.5 Listening

Listen to the conversation and answer these questions.

1 Barbara would work for

  a a company with a bad pollution record.
  b a nuclear waste disposal company.
  c a company that makes profits out of the Third World.

2 In question 2, the employee says it is OK for him to make a lot of calls because

  a the company makes a lot of money.
  b he makes a lot of money for the company.
  c the calls do not cost a lot of money.

3 Barbara does not agree with the employee's attitude because

  a you are not paid to make calls.
  b the calls cost too much money.
  c the company pays you for the work you do.

4 What percentage of people said they would work for a nuclear disposal company?

  a 14 per cent b 55 per cent c 45 per cent

5 In question two, what percentage of people disagreed with the employee's attitude?

  a 18 per cent b 80 per cent c 5 per cent

Key and tapescripts

1.1

1 2 What do you do?
   3 Who do you work for?
   4 Where are you from?
   5 Where do you live?

2 2d 3a 4c 5e

3 📼 ⊙

MICHAEL: Hello, Andrea, how are you?
ANDREA: Hello, Michael, I'm fine thanks. How are you?
MICHAEL: Not too bad. Did you have a good flight?
ANDREA: Yes, thanks, although it was a little rough.
MICHAEL: How are things at head office?
ANDREA: We've been really busy, I think we're going to have a very good year!

1.2

1 2e 3a 4b 5d

2 2 When did you arrive?
   3 Where are you staying?
   4 Did you come to the office by taxi?
   5 How long are you staying?
   6 Would you like anything to drink?

3 Susan seems very rude. She does not try to keep the conversation going. She could have had a long journey, but when meeting a business associate she should still try to be polite.

📼 ⊙

A: Hello, Susan, welcome to Melbourne.
B: Hello.
A: Did you have a good flight?
B: Yes.
A: Have you got a lot of baggage?
B: Yes.
A: Oh. I've booked a taxi to take us to your hotel.
B: I'd rather take the bus.

Suggested answer

A: Hello, Susan, welcome to Melbourne.
B: Hello, David. Nice to see you again.
A: Did you have a good flight?
B: Yes. But I'm very tired, it's a long way from Chicago!
A: Have you got a lot of baggage?
B: Yes.
A: I've booked a taxi to take us to your hotel.
B: Oh, thanks. That's better than the bus!

1.3

1 1 F It reports Japanese news stories in English.
2 F It reports news stories from Japanese newspapers and magazines. 3 T 4 F We are not told how many people read it. 3,000,000 read *Nihon Keizai Shimbun*.

2 2f 3a 4d 5b 6e

3 Tick statements 2 and 4.

   1 No, she left the company.
   3 No, she did work there.
   5 No, they met at Lear's.

📼 ⊙

A: That's Vikkie Behle over there, isn't it?
B: No, it isn't. Vikkie left the company last year. That's her replacement, Carol Simms.
A: I thought I recognized her. She used to work at Jones's, didn't she?
B: That's right. She worked there for five years, didn't she?
A: No, I think it was only three years. Before that, she worked at Lear's.
B: Vikkie Behle once worked there, didn't she?
A: Yes. That's where Carol met Vikkie. It's a small world, isn't it!

2.1

1 1 It is in the pharmaceutical business.
2 It manufactures and markets drugs.
3 The United States.

2 2 What line of business are you in?
3 What do you make/produce?
4 Where are your headquarters?
5 Where are your main markets?
6 How many employees do you have?/
How many people do you employ?

2.2

1 1a 2d 3e 4b 5f 6c

Well, after I left school … that was in 1984 … I went to Paris for a year to learn French. When I came back to England I did a bilingual secretarial course and then I moved to Australia. I went to live in Brisbane and in 1986 I opened a sandwich bar for office workers. It was a great success – not only were our sandwiches better than anyone else's, we were one of the first to offer a delivery service … and I suppose that was when I developed a taste for business.
My mother died towards the end of 1988 and the following year, 1989, I went back to England to take over her business, which supplied London restaurants with fish. I ran that business for five years, but eventually sold it in 1994 because by that time my own business was doing well. That all started because when Christmas came I found I needed gifts for the customers my mother had been supplying. I hit on the idea of giving them fish motif cufflinks I'd designed and, well, I've never looked back since.

2 1 be 2 become 3 begin 4 do 5 get
6 go 7 have 8 leave 9 make 10 say
11 sell 12 take

3 1b 2c 3a 4e 5f 6d 7 main office
8 annual turnover 9 regional branches
10 employ 80 staff

2.3

1

17 Glendale Road
Glasgow G14 1RU
Scotland

Electrostir
Orchard Street,
Ashford,
Kent TN10 1AH

21 November 199–

Dear Sir or Madam

I saw your advertisement in the November issue of LABORATORY NEWS and am interested in your range of products.

Could you please send me a catalogue and price list together with information regarding discounts.

I look forward to hearing from you.

Yours sincerely

Henry Koh

2

Call 1

Louise Nevelson
Parkeston Quay
Harwich
Essex CO12 7RS

Call 2

Simon Wright
2258 Rutherford Road
Carlsbad, California
92008
USA

Call 1

WOMAN: And my address is Parkeston Quay, Harwich. I'll spell that. That's P.A.R.K.E.S.T.O.N. Quay, that's Q.U.A.Y. New line. Harwich. That's H.A.R.W.I.C.H. Essex. And the postcode is CO12 7RS. I'll just repeat that. CO12 7RS.

Call 2

MAN: Could you send it to 2258 Rutherford Road, Carlsbad, California. Rutherford. That's R.U.T.H.E.R.F.O.R.D. Carlsbad. That's C.A.R.L.S.B.A.D. California. Zip code 92008. USA. Thank you very much.

3 2 Certainly. Could I have your name and address, please?
3 I'm sorry. Could you repeat that?
4 Could you spell Choudhry?
5 Could I have your address?
6 Of course, Ms Choudhry. I'll post our catalogue to you today.

Unit 3

3.1

1 2e 3b 4c 5f 6a 7 leading suppliers
8 successful applicant 9 keyboard skills
10 attractive salary

2 1f 2d 3c 4a 5e 6b

3

		7					
1	T	R	A	V	E	L	
	2	S	A	L	A	R	Y
	3	C	L	E	R	K	
		A					
4	B	E	N	E	F	I	T	S
	5	C	E	O			
6	A	P	P	L	Y		

3.2

1 2E 3T 4E 5E 6E 7E 8T 9T 10T
11T

2

I work in the Dispatch department. We send goods to customers. At the moment we're very busy because we are packing machines for a trade fair next week.
This is my colleague. She works in the Export department. She answers customers' enquiries about our products and sends them information. This week she is helping me prepare for the fair.

3.3

1 1b 2e 3c 4f 5a 6d

2 Call 1

For: Kate North
From: Peter Coghlan
Message: Please call back on 261 5000 about your order.

Call 2

For: Wendy West
From: Andy Collins
Message: Please call back on 171 6145 before 5 this afternoon.

Call 1

WOMAN: Gizmo Gadgets. Good morning.
MAN 1: This is Peter Coghlan from Printkwik. Could I speak to Kate North, please?
WOMAN: Hold the line please … Hello? I'm afraid there's no reply. Would you like to leave a message?
MAN 1: Er, yes. Could you ask her to call me back about her order?
WOMAN: Right. Could I have your name and number?
MAN 1: Sure. My name's Coghlan. That's C.O.G.H.L.A.N. And my number's 261 5000.
WOMAN: I'll just repeat that. Mr Coghlan on 261 5000. OK. Thank you for calling.
MAN 1: Thank you. Goodbye.

Call 2

WOMAN: Gizmo gadgets. Good morning.
MAN 2: This is Andy Collins. I'd like to speak to Wendy West please.
WOMAN: She's in a meeting. Can I take a message?
MAN 2: Er, yes. Could you ask her to call me back sometime today? I'll be in my office until about 5 this afternoon.
WOMAN: Right. Could I have your name and number?
MAN 2: Sure. Andy Collins. And my number's 171 6145.
WOMAN: I'll just repeat that. Mr Collins on 171 6145. Call back before 5 o'clock. Right, Mr Collins. I'll ask her to call you when she comes out of the meeting.
MAN 2: Thank you. Goodbye.

3 2 I'm sorry, he's in a meeting.
3 I'm sorry, I don't know. Can I take a message?
4 Of course. Who's calling, please?
5 Could I have your number, please?
6 OK. Ms Salcini. I'll ask him to call you when he gets in.

Unit 4

4.1

1 a Greece   b France/Germany
c Holland/Greece   d Italy

2 ▭ ◉

1

VOICE 1: dinner tonight (*beep*)
(*pause*)
VOICE 2: Would you like to have dinner tonight?
(*pause*)
VOICE 2: Would you like to have dinner tonight?

2

VOICE 1: sightseeing on Saturday (*beep*)
VOICE 2: Would you like to go sightseeing on Saturday?
VOICE 2: Would you like to go sightseeing on Saturday?

3

VOICE 1: have a game of tennis tomorrow (*beep*)
VOICE 2: Would you like to have a game of tennis tomorrow?
VOICE 2: Would you like to have a game of tennis tomorrow?

VOICE 1: Now use *How about …?*

4

VOICE 1: go out for lunch today (*beep*)
VOICE 2: How about going out for lunch today?
VOICE 2: How about going out for lunch today?

5

VOICE 1: play a round of golf at the weekend (*beep*)
VOICE 2: How about playing a round of golf at the weekend?
VOICE 2: How about playing a round of golf at the weekend?

3 Suggested answers

1 A: I hear you play tennis. Would you like a game this evening?
B: *I'm afraid I'm having dinner with a friend tonight.*
A: That's a pity. How about tomorrow evening?
B: *That would be fine.*

2 A: Would you like to watch a game of German football? Dortmund is playing Bayern München on Saturday.
B: *I'd love to. What time is the match?*
A: It starts at three. I'll pick you up at your hotel.
B: *That's very kind of you. I'll look forward to it.*

4.2

1 Books: novel, biography, science fiction, crime, thriller
Films: western, horror, comedy, science fiction, thriller
Music: classical, jazz, soul, pop

2 1d   2b   3f   4c   5e   6a

4.3

1 ▭ ◉

The correct answers are in *italics*.

Time on their hands
Europeans work fewer hours for more money. So what do they do with their time? In the cold, grey north they watch TV. Denmark has *386* sets for every 1,000 people, Germany has *385*. In sunny Spain they eat out: *14 per cent* of household spending goes on restaurants, cafés and hotels. Europeans everywhere watch football. One in *three* is interested in football, one in *four* in tennis and swimming and one in *five* in athletics and gymnastics.
Above all, the newly rich Europeans go on holiday. *34 per cent* take their main holidays in August and another *28 per cent* in July. For peace (if not sun) try February or November, when only *1 per cent* take their main holiday. *50 per cent* of Europe's holidaymakers head for the seaside. But in Holland people prefer a holiday in the countryside to a week on the beach.

2 1 They watch television.
2 They eat out.
3 Football.
4 Tennis, swimming, athletics, gymnastics.
5 In July and August.
6 At the seaside.

3

always		frequently		sometimes		never
	regularly		often		seldom	

Progress test 1

5.1

1 works   2 answers   3 deals   4 prepares
5 is preparing   6 is organizing   7 is writing

5.2

1 leading supplier
2 main office
3 regional branches
4 employs (80) staff
5 annual turnover

5.3

1 don't you
2 doesn't she
3 isn't he
4 don't they
5 does she

5.4

Suggested answers

FRIEND: Would you *like to have a game of tennis tonight?*

YOU: I'm afraid *I'm having dinner with a client this evening.*

FRIEND: *Well, would you like to have a game tomorrow night?*

YOU: I'm sorry, *I'm going to Rome on business tomorrow and I won't be back until quite late.* How about *Thursday evening?*

FRIEND: Thursday would be fine. *Would 7 o'clock be OK?*

YOU: Seven o'clock would be fine. I'll see you then. Bye for now.

FRIEND: Bye.

5.5

1 began   2 became   3 started   4 made
5 took   6 sold

5.6

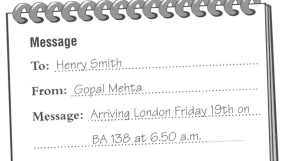

Message

To: Henry Smith

From: Gopal Mehta

Message: Arriving London Friday 19th on
BA 138 at 6.50 a.m.

RECEPTIONIST: Hello, Industrial Plastics International. Can I help you?

MEHTA: Hello, this is Gopal Mehta calling from Mumbai. Could I speak to Henry Smith please?

RECEPTIONIST: I'll try for you … There's no reply, could I take a message?

MEHTA: Yes. Please tell him that I called.

RECEPTIONIST: Sorry. Could I have your name again, please?

MEHTA: Certainly. It's Gopal Mehta. That's G.O.P.A.L. Mehta, that's M.E.H.T.A.

RECEPTIONIST: Gopal Mehta. Yes.

MEHTA: And I'm arriving in London on Friday the 19th at 6.50 a.m. on BA 138.

RECEPTIONIST: Arriving Friday the 19th on BA 138. Sorry, what was the time again?

MEHTA: 6.50 a.m.

RECEPTIONIST: 6.50 a.m. OK, Mr Mehta, I'll see that he gets the message. Thank you for calling.

MEHTA: Thank you. Goodbye.

RECEPTIONIST: Goodbye.

Unit 6

6.1

1 1c   2d   3b   4f   5e   6a

2 1f   2a   3c   4b   5e   6d

INTERVIEWER: I understand that your company is looking to expand overseas. Could you tell us what you look for when considering a location?

WOMAN: Of course. One of the most important things for us is that there is good transportation available. We are a global company, so we need to be somewhere where our staff can reach our other offices by direct flights. We must also be able to ship our goods out, so again we need good sea, rail and air links to export our products. Communications are also very important: good telephone services are essential, and we are also relying more and more on electronic forms of communication.

INTERVIEWER: Once you've found a place that satisfies these requirements, what would be your next priority?

WOMAN: For manufacturing, we need modern, high-quality factories with the latest equipment, so that would be our next consideration. And for our office-based staff, we need modern, efficient and comfortable offices. So the availability of good commercial premises is very important. Also essential are good services so that if a machine breaks down we can get it repaired quickly and easily.

INTERVIEWER: What else is important in making your decision?

WOMAN: Well, to manufacture to the highest standards, we need to have a well educated, well trained workforce available – human resources are a key to success. No point in setting up an operation if the people are not there to do the job! And, of course, as staff from our other offices are sometimes moved in to help set up the operation, we need somewhere that can provide them with a variety of comfortable housing, good shopping and all the comforts and services that people today expect, so a good standard of living is also important.

3 1 airport 2 rail 3 goods trains 4 lorry
5 container 6 port 7 cargo ship

6.2

1 1 T 2 F It now takes 32 hours by train, a full day less than by road. 3 T 4 T

2 Suggested answers

2 Road transport is not as safe as rail.
3 It's faster than road transport.
4 It's much more flexible than sea transport.
5 It's more economical than air transport.

3

					6				
1	L	I	V	E	S	T	O	C	K
		2	F	L	A	M	M	A	B	L	E
		3	P	E	R	I	S	H	A	B	L	E
		4	F	R	A	G	I	L	E
5	H	A	Z	A	R	D	O	U	S

6.3

1 1 Ms Sanchez, Royale Engineering
2 9.50 a.m. on 15 September
3 2
4 1380
5 5
6 1935
7 Ms Sanchez
8 Royale Engineering
9 air

Hello, Mr Davison. This is Ms Sanchez at Royale Engineering. I'm calling you at 9.50 a.m. on 15 September. Thank you for delivering the last order so quickly. I need to place an urgent order with you. We need 2 units of model 1380 and 5 units of model 1935. That's 2 of model 1380 and 5 of model 1935. Please send them to me at Royale Engineering by air. We do not require insurance, and we will pay for the cost of transport as it is so urgent.

3 Suggested answer

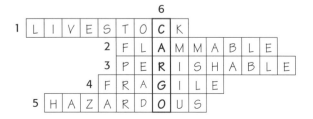

V A C Industries

From: Brian Davison
To: Dispatch Department
Date: 15 September

Goods details

Units	Model
3	1380
4	1935

Shipping details

Please send the above order by sea to Ms Sanchez at Royale Engineering. They do not need insurance, and we will pay for sea transport.

Unit 7

7.1

1 1 Australia 2 Switzerland 3 Brazil

2 Total earnings:

6%: Agriculture

31%: Industry

63%: Services

Exports (in billions of US$):

Fruit and vegetables: 3.6

Processed foods: 2.6

Livestock: 2.1

Minerals: 2.2

Argentina has a strong economy based on its rich agricultural and mineral resources and its thriving service industry. Agriculture accounted for 6 per cent of the country's total income last year. Much of this was exported, and earned the country 3.6 billion dollars for fruit and vegetable products, 2.6 billion for processed foods and 2.1 billion for livestock. The country also exported 2.2 billion dollars worth of minerals. Total export earnings were 21 billion dollars. Industry accounted for 31 per cent of total earnings last year, and services accounted for 63 per cent. Brazil was the biggest export destination, with over 25 per cent of all goods going there. By contrast, the United States was the major supplier of imports, accounting for 21 per cent of imports last year.

3

```
                6
                A
                U
      1 T E X T I L E
            2 C O M P U T E R
  3 T O U R I S M
        4 P E T R O L E U M
                B
                I
  5 A G R I C U L T U R E
                E
```

7.2

1 Suggested answers

2 How many tractors do you import?

3 How much coffee do you import?

4 How much steel do you import?

5 How many textiles do you import?

6 How much wheat do you import?

2 Suggested answers

2 They export many automobiles.

3 They export some chemicals.

4 They export a little coal.

5 They export much steel.

6 They export a lot of sugar.

3

The largest export for this country is petroleum, while the smallest is computers. Financial and insurance services contribute 13 per cent and tourism contributes 15 per cent. Fertile land and good rainfall, together with a warm climate, make agriculture a major earner for the economy (20 per cent). Suitable conditions for sheep and good cotton-growing areas make textiles the third largest contributor to the economy.

7.3

1 1c   2b   3a   4b

2 2 knew

3 has been

4 have become

5 have begun

6 has improved

3 Suggested answer

When it started it served 18 destinations, but the number has increased to 45. In 1988 there was only one class of service, but now West Air has introduced a new business class. There were no airport lounges in 1988. Now West Air has begun to provide lounges in all major airports.

Unit 8

8.1

1 1 are meeting

2 is flying

3 will phone

4 will send

5 am going

6 will take

2

1

VOICE 1: I'm arriving on … (*beep*)

(*pause*)

VOICE 2: When are you arriving?

(*pause*)

VOICE 2: When are you arriving?

2

VOICE 1: I'm staying at … (*beep*)

VOICE 2: Where are you staying?

VOICE 2: Where are you staying?

3

VOICE 1: On Tuesday I'm seeing Mr … (*beep*)

VOICE 2: Who are you seeing on Tuesday?

VOICE 2: Who are you seeing on Tuesday?

4

VOICE 1: I'm meeting him to … (*beep*)
VOICE 2: Why are you meeting him?
VOICE 2: Why are you meeting him?

5

VOICE 1: I'm … on Wednesday morning. (*beep*)
VOICE 2: What are you doing on Wednesday morning?
VOICE 2: What are you doing on Wednesday morning?

8.2

1 2e 3b 4f 5c 6a
  7 attend (the) conference
  8 enclose (my) registration form
  9 book a room
  10 reserve a table
  Note: Book: to make an arrangement for something (such as a seat or a table) at a particular time. Reserve: to arrange for something to be kept for you. In this exercise, 'confirm' could also be used with e, confirm a reservation.

2 1e 2c 3a 4d 5f 6b

3 Suggested answer

  1

> Dear Mr Howard
>
> Thank you for your invitation to the launch of your new range. I am afraid that I will not be able to come as I have to travel to Paris that evening.
>
> Yours sincerely

  2

> Dear Ms Smith
>
> Thank you for your invitation to view Infotel's new range of software on Monday, 29 January. I will be pleased to attend.
>
> Yours sincerely

8.3

1 Tuesday   meet Helen at **10**
  Thursday   Fly to **Melbourne**
  Friday   Tour new **factory**

HELEN: Hello, Paul. It's Helen here. How are you?
PAUL: Fine thanks, a bit busy.
HELEN: What's up?
PAUL: Well, I'm going to Melbourne next week to see the new factory. I'm flying there on Thursday, and seeing the new building on Friday.
HELEN: That's going to be quite a trip.
PAUL: Yes, and there's a lot to do before I go. On Monday I'm attending a computer course all day. And on Tuesday the Sales Manager wants to have lunch with me. And on Wednesday, there are four applicants to be interviewed for the Sales Assistant position!
HELEN: Well, you certainly sound busy. I'm sorry but I've actually called to try to see you about the Sales Report. Is there any time left in your diary for next week?
PAUL: I could see you Tuesday morning – about 10?
HELEN: Ten would be fine. See you then.
PAUL: Bye.

2 Suggested answers

  2 He's seeing Helen about the Sales Report on Tuesday morning.
  3 He's having lunch with the Sales Manager on Tuesday.
  4 He's interviewing applicants on Wednesday.
  5 He's flying to Melbourne on Thursday.
  6 He's seeing the new factory on Friday.

3 1a 2e 3g 4b 5h 6f 7d 8i 9c

Unit 9

9.1

1 1/2 deposit cheques / withdraw cash
  3 pay bills
  4 borrow money
  5 order (your) traveller's cheques

2

BANK: Hello, First Direct, how can I help you?
CUSTOMER: I'd like to find out some prices for foreign currency.
BANK: Of course. Which currencies are you interested in?

CUSTOMER: US dollars and Japanese Yen.

BANK: Today's rate is US$1.64 to the pound. For the Yen it's 210.65 to the pound. Is there anything else I can help you with?

CUSTOMER: No, that's all. Thank you for your help.

BANK: Thank you for calling.

3 Suggested answer

First Direct provides a 24-hours a day, seven days a week service. You can do all your banking by phone, including paying your bills. They pay a good rate of interest, and you can withdraw cash at thousands of cash machines.

9.2

1

1 This chest of drawers is **160 cm** high.
2 It measures **84 × 40 × 90 cm**.
3 It's got **8** drawers.
4 It costs **$349**.
5 Postage and packing is an extra **$6.90**.
6 The order number is **1976–32**.

2 2 How many shelves has it got?
3 What's it made of?
4 How much does it weigh?
5 How much does it cost?
6 Does that include delivery? / Is delivery included?

3 1f 2e 3c 4b 5d 6a

9.3

1 1c 2b 3c 4a 5b

We decided to put an emphasis on customer service because Foodliner is a small supermarket. There's a lot of competition from much larger stores owned by the big chains. The first thing we did was to cut waiting time at the checkouts. We now have an average waiting time of three minutes and a maximum of five minutes. That's pretty good compared to the delays at our rivals. We've also introduced a bus service once a week to bring in customers without cars. We've worked hard to provide good service for the disabled. Our store is designed for wheelchairs, and our staff will make up orders for disabled customers or, if they want, accompany them around the store.

We train our staff to be welcoming and friendly, although it's very important to recruit the right people in the beginning. We have a low turnover of staff, which means they can be brought into the family way of doing business.

We hope to have loyal customers, who over the years will spend large sums of money at our store. After all, existing customers are easier to reach than new ones. And satisfied customers promote for free.

2 Suggested answers

1 ... a good customer
2 ... the soap he likes
3 ... ten minutes to pay for his shopping
4 ... the bus home
5 ... somewhere else if this happens again

3 Suggested answer

Dear Mr Beasley

Thank you for your letter. I am very sorry to hear about the problems you had when you came to our store last week.

First of all, please let me know what brand of soap you wanted. We will supply you with 10 bars of this soap free of charge.

I am sorry about the wait at the checkout. One of our staff was sick that day, and one of the tills was being repaired, so we had problems serving our customers as quickly as we would like to. We certainly hope that this will not happen again.

Finally, I am sorry that you missed our bus service. If you travelled home by taxi with your shopping, we would be pleased to pay you for the taxi ride. Again, please let me know how much it cost you.

We are very sorry that you were unhappy when you shopped with us last week, and we would not like to lose you as our customer. We hope that you are satisfied with what I have suggested above.

Yours sincerely

Customer Relations
Foodliner

Progress test 2

10.1

1 started
2 flew
3 used
4 has grown
5 has carried
6 served
7 took
8 has grown

10.2

1 Transporting goods by air is faster than by sea.
2 Travelling by air is less environmentally friendly than by train.
3 Sending perishable goods by rail is worse than by air.

10.3

1 Could you / Please send me a copy of your brochure.
2 I'm afraid / Unfortunately I cannot / am unable to attend the meeting.
3 I am writing to / I would like to confirm our meeting next week.
4 Thank you for dinner / your hospitality last week.
5 Thank you for your invitation. I would be most pleased to attend the conference.
6 I would like to arrange a meeting for next Thursday.

10.4

1 textile
2 cotton
3 petroleum
4 coffee
5 agricultural
6 automobiles
7 consumer electronics
8 service
9/10 banking / tourism

10.5

1 I'm flying to Kuala Lumpur on Thursday. Please book a hotel room.
2 OK, I'll book a hotel.
3 I'm staying four nights. Then I'm going to Singapore. Please send a fax to the office there.
4 Fine. I'll send a fax to the Singapore office.
5 I am meeting Mr Bandur there. Please send a report to him.
6 Yes, I'll send a report to him.

10.6

1 China exports a lot of machinery.
2 China exports quite a lot of chemicals.
3 China exports a few vehicles.
4 China exports a little oil.

10.7

Name:	Shirley Wang	
Company:	Intertel	
Model		**Units**
S 132		18
M813		32
Send by (tick): Sea ☐ Air ✓		

Hello, this is Shirley Wang, that's S.H.I.R.L.E.Y, Shirley, Wang, W.A.N.G. I'm calling from Intertel, that's I.N.T.E.R.T.E.L in Taipei. I would like to order the following items: 18 units of model S132 and 32 units of M813. That's 18 of S132 and 32 of M813. The last order was sent by sea and it arrived late, so please send this order by air. Thank you.

Unit 11

11.1

1 1 The new logo is blue.
2 The colour suggests stability and reliability and projects a warm and intimate feeling.
3 It's easier to read and to remember.
4 The shape symbolizes the world moving through space.
5 They show Samsung's desire to be one with the world and to serve society.

2 1b 2d 3a 4f 5e 6c

In business we rely on paper to communicate. But do you ever stop to think about what the paper itself says? Today, I'm going to be talking about using coloured paper to improve your business image.
Now, as you know, white is the colour most commonly used in business writing paper. But there is no reason why you should not use other colours. The effects of these colours have been researched and I'd like to tell you something about them.

Let's start by looking at blue, a colour which is thought to express confidence and harmony. The next colour in the spectrum is green. Now if you wish to suggest life and growth, green is the colour of choice. Next is yellow, which, as you can imagine, communicates cheerfulness. Red is the ideal colour if you wish to convey activity and excitement. Grey, often overlooked, suggests age, wisdom and judgement. Purple is a difficult colour to use because it can stand for tradition and staleness, not necessarily an image you want for your company!

3 2a 3e 4c 5d

11.2

1 1b 2d 3c 4a

2 1 How many consumers buy a product after seeing it in television ads?
2 What was the first product that was distributed?
3 How many samples were distributed to households last year?
4 When was sampling first used in Britain?

3

```
          8
    1 S P E C I A L
  2 D I R E C T
    3 O F F E R
    4 M A I L
  5 C O N S U M E R
6 A D V E R T I S I N G
          I
          O
    7 P E N
```

11.3

1 1 91048
2 951-846
3 White
4 45p
5 970-482
6 250
7 £1.89
8 Print name on items

SALESPERSON: Promotions Plus. Good morning.
RENZO: Hello, this is Renzo from Moda Sportswear. I'd like to place an order for some merchandising material.
SALESPERSON: Hello, Renzo. Could I have your customer number, please?
RENZO: Yes. It's 91048.
SALESPERSON: 91048. Just a minute … Right. What would you like to order?

RENZO: I'd like 600 ballpoint pens at 45p each, catalogue number 951-846. And then catalogue number 970-482, 250 baseball caps at £1.89 each. Both in white.
SALESPERSON: I'll just read that back. 600 ballpoint pens, catalogue number 951-846. And 250 baseball caps, catalogue number 970-482. Anything else?
RENZO: No, that's all. But we'd like the company name printed on both items.
SALESPERSON: Right. Well, we'll need film for that.
RENZO: Er, it's actually a repeat order, so I think you should have it.
SALESPERSON: OK, I'll make a note of that. If we can find the film, then your goods should be ready in a couple of weeks. Is that all right?
RENZO: Yes, that's fine. Thanks very much.
SALESPERSON: You're welcome. Goodbye.

2 / 3

> **Promotions Plus**
> Unit 15
> Bedford Industrial Estate
> Stevenage
> Herts SG11 1PN
>
> Moda Sportswear
> 34 Rose Street
> Edinburgh EH1 1HZ
>
> Dear Renzo
> Thank you for your recent order (2) for merchandising items. (5)
>
> We are pleased to confirm your order for ballpoint pens and (4) baseball caps printed with your company name. (8)
>
> We look forward to hearing (1) that the goods have arrived safely (6) and to doing (3) business with you in future. (7)
>
> Yours sincerely
>
> Promotions Plus

Unit 12

12.1

1 1 a sudden collapse   2 a slight increase
3 a steady decline   4 a dramatic rise
5 a gradual rise   6 a jump

2 1 gradually   2 sharp   3 slight   4 slowly
5 strongly

3 1 soared   2 climbed   3 plunged   4 declined
5 remained stable

12.2

1 1 Eastern Europe
2 Africa
3 China
4 Pacific
5 Latin America
6 Asia

2 Suggested answers

1 The new Elantra model was successful because
of Hyundai's good reputation.
2 Overall sales grew as a result of Hyundai
exporting to new markets.
3 African sales should rise as a result of new
plants being built in Egypt, Botswana and
Zimbabwe.
4 By 2000, Hyundai's overseas production will
reach 500,000 vehicles a year due to world-
wide demand for its vehicles.

3 1b   2c   3c   4a   5b

Hyundai has a major programme for overseas
expansion, with eight overseas assembly plants at
planning stage or under construction. In 1996
construction of its new plant in India started. In
the first stage, Hyundai will invest US$700 million
and will produce 100,000 cars every year. Initially
the factory will produce smaller cars for India's
young buyers. Cars produced at this factory will
be ready for market in 1998. In the second stage,
Hyundai will invest another US$400 million to
increase production to 200,000 vehicles per year.
Hyundai also has plants planned or under
construction in Turkey, Pakistan, Malaysia, Vietnam
and Taiwan, plus a factory just starting operation
in Venezuela.

12.3

1 1d   2b   3c   4a

2 1b   2e   3a   4c   5d

3 Part 1: 1 T   2 F It was long and terrible.   3 T
Part 2: Tick statements b, d, e and f

Part 1

Some years ago I was invited to give a 90 minute
presentation. The memory of arriving and
standing before those who had paid to listen to
me still gives me nightmares.

I realized the minute I stepped on stage that I was
not prepared. The audience knew that, and they
also knew more about my subject than I ever
would.
The first 15 minutes were long and terrible.
Several members of the audience actually left the
room. I remember thinking I would be very lucky
to survive 45 minutes.
I only just made it. I tried everything to save the
situation. I asked the audience to take part, to
share their experiences, to ask questions. Nothing
worked. I finished halfway through and went back
to my hotel.

Part 2

Later, I thought about why I did it so badly and
what I could do in future.
The first problem was that I cared more about
what I wanted to say than what the audience
wanted to hear. So ask yourself who the audience
is and what they want.
The second problem was I didn't have enough
material. You must have at least three times as
much as you will need – something might go
wrong and you will need that extra material.
The third problem was that I didn't prepare
enough. It takes 60 minutes of preparation for
every 5 minutes of your presentation, together
with three full rehearsals.
Now I always work very hard at presentations and
make sure no corners have been cut.

Unit 13

13.1

1 Tick statements 1, 3 and 5
2 It's often easier to sell in bad weather.
4 No, it stops them buying from you.

2 1c   2b   3d   4a

13.2

1 *Part 1*
1 because they have no money
2 7.5 per cent
3 12 months / a year

Part 2

4 30 days
5 51 days
6 £70,000 to £80,000 a year

Part 1

It's January and I'm still waiting for payment on
many deliveries, some from September, a few from

May. Usually you get excuses, but now I'm getting honest answers – Sorry, we don't have any money. How can you get money out of people who have none? We're offering a 7.5 per cent discount for prompt payment, but none of our slow payers have taken it, they're just too short of cash. I reckon I can survive another 12 months like this. I have a friend who has been very successful in business – he's a millionaire. His advice to me was 'Don't play banker to other businesses'. He's right, but what can I do? I'm just a small supplier.

Part 2

About 6 months ago we noticed trade debtors extending the number of days they owed our company money. The agreement on our invoices is the standard 30 days. We used to be paid on average within 45 days, but now it takes 51. That extra 5 or 6 days will cost us a total of £70,000 to £80,000 over a year. Now, we have a tighter credit control system. We chase customers for payment before the 30 days are up, not 45 days after delivery.

2 Suggested answers

1 If a customer has a bad credit record, don't give them credit.
2 If someone promises payment and it doesn't come, chase it immediately.
3 Ask a debt collector for help if a customer refuses to pay.
4 If you want prompt payment, make sure that your invoices are correct.

3 1 Invoices
2 overdue
3 chasing
4 reminders
5 credit
6 collect

13.3

1 1a [C] →2d [S] →3e [S] →4b [S] →5c [S]
→6f [C]

2 Call 1

From: Sarah Watkins
Company: HyperTech
Invoice number: 187–956
Message: Their order was incomplete. They will pay as soon as they receive the missing goods.

Call 2

From: Arnold Simms
Company: WordText
Invoice number: ZQ48-OH
Message: They will pay as soon as we send them a correct invoice.

Call 1

Hello, this is Sarah Watkins from HyperTech. We received your reminder this morning about invoice number 187-956. Unfortunately, the order was incomplete. We are still waiting for the missing goods. We promise to pay immediately once we receive them.

Call 2

Hi, this is Arnold Simms from WordText. Thanks for your reminder about invoice ZQ48-OH. I called you about this last week. The first invoice you sent had a mistake in it. Please send us a new invoice and we will pay it without delay.

3 2f 3a 4e 5b 6d

Unit 14

14.1

1 Tick statement 2
1 No, they often remember days or weeks after the occasion.
3 They *may* write one.
4 Only take *one* gift.

For Americans, the fact that they remember an occasion such as a birthday or anniversary at all makes them feel good. The present may come days or even weeks late, but everyone will feel happy that the occasion has been marked. You should wrap gifts and include a handwritten note, which Americans read before opening the gift. They open gifts immediately, and will then describe their pleasure at receiving it. The gift is often passed around for others to admire. Sometime later you may receive a note of appreciation.

When invited to a home in the United States, bring a bottle of wine or flowers. A small item of home decoration from your country is also appreciated. But remember, you shouldn't take wine, flowers and a gift – just choose one.

2 1a 2c 3b 4c

14.2

1 1 No, they are often lonely and bored.
2 Safety and security are worries, and dining alone can be unpleasant. Many hotels are only equipped for businessmen and lack things that women need such as skirt hangers.
3 Diane Newhofer.
4 Women who travel on business can become members.
5 It provides information about hotels, gyms, restaurants and bars for women travelling alone. It puts members in touch with each other so they can meet when they are away from home.

2 Could you tell me / Do you know …
2 where I can change money?
3 what time the bank opens?
4 where the business centre is?
5 what number bus I need to get to the exhibition centre?
6 how often the bus to the exhibition centre runs?

3 1e 2a 3c 4d 5b 6g 7f

14.3

1 Tick statements 2, 3, 6 and 8.
1 Doesn't say.
4 Some socializing is acceptable.
5 Dinners are more popular.
7 They go on very late.

Part 1
If we want to entertain business clients in the States, we'll invite them to a business lunch. Business breakfasts are also popular. A serious lunch will last for a maximum of two hours and will be sometime between 12 and 3. We usually have three courses: an appetizer, a main course and a dessert followed by coffee. You can certainly discuss business over lunch, although of course you do also need to socialize.

Part 2
Business lunches are quite common in Korea, although it is more common to have a business dinner which is usually followed up with a lot of drinking. This is at a nice sit-down bar or Karaoke bar. These business dinners usually last until late

evening or early morning and are a way of getting to know each other better. Business can be discussed at any time during the dinner or afterwards while drinking.

2 1d 2b 3a 4e 5c

3

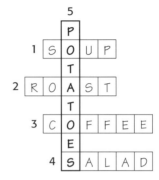

Progress test 3

15.1

1 plunged   2 decreased   3 climbed/rose
4 soared   5 increased   6 fell
7 rose/climbed

15.2

1 Could you tell me where the train station is?
2 Do you know what time the bus leaves?
3 Could you tell me when the shops close today?
4 How do I get to the conference centre?
5 When is breakfast served?
6 What is the restaurant's phone number?

15.3

1 sharply   2 steady   3 sharp
4 dramatically   5 steadily   6 slow

15.4

Suggested answers
1 A Credit Controller is someone who checks that invoices are paid.
2 First Direct is a bank which has no branches.
3 Oil is a product which Mexico exports.
4 Computers are machines which help businesses.
5 A programmer is someone who writes computer programs.

15.5

Cooking methods	Meats	Vegetables
fry	beef	salad
grill	lamb	beans
roast	pork	Brussels sprouts
boil	chicken	spinach
steam	ham	potatoes

15.6

1 If sales do not improve, we won't make a profit.
2 If profits are high, we will get a pay increase.
3 I will lower the price if you pay cash.
4 If you take 10,000, we'll give you a discount.
5 We'll give you 60 days' credit if you pay for delivery.

15.7

1b 2c 3a, c 4b, c

INTERVIEWER: First of all, could you tell me something about why you decided to change your company's image?

SPOKESPERSON: Well, we had been receiving some bad publicity about one of our health care products. Journalists thought that we were just trying to scare people into using this product, and that it was all rather silly. So we thought that we needed a fresh approach, a more modern, serious look.

INTERVIEWER: How did you go about developing the new identity?

SPOKESPERSON: Well, at first we wanted a design to show we are a company with many different services. But it was difficult to find good symbols for all our activities. We did want to change the company colour, but we didn't want to change our name. There were a lot of different choices and decisions to make.

INTERVIEWER: How long did it take to change your logo?

SPOKESPERSON: About 18 months. It's quite a big job as you have to advertise the change so people know what's happening, you have to repaint vehicles, you need new office supplies with the name and logo on them – the list of things we had to change was long and rather surprising!

INTERVIEWER: And has it been successful?

SPOKESPERSON: Now that the change is complete, the company does feel that it was worth it. Our image is much stronger and the change in itself has brought good publicity.

Unit 16

16.1

1 1 Germany 2 France 3 Sweden / Switzerland
4 Italy 5 Britain

2

```
                    6
                    M
        1 W A R E H O U S E
                    N
     2 O V E R A L L S
                    A
                    G
        3 P R E V I O U S
                    M
     4 E X E C U T I V E
                    N
                5 S T A F F
```

16.2

1 1 computer software
2 expense account / personal calls
3 confidential report
4 office supplies

2 1T 2F Her family call her. 3F They live in another state. 4 T 5 T 6 T

WOMAN: I work in an office that has an 800 number for customers, you know, a number that customers can use to call us on and we pay for the call. I have a bit of a problem with a colleague of mine. Anyway, she sits near me and because I often have to answer her phone, I know she's misusing this 800 number. You see, what she does is she gets her family to call her on it. And they live in another state, so this is costing the company a lot of money. And her supervisor has no idea what's going on. I don't know whether I should tell her or not …

MAN: I've had similar problems at work. A few months ago the head of my department invited a group of us out to lunch after we'd finished a big project. Well, we had a great meal and then, afterwards, we all chipped in $10. Our boss collected the money and then paid the bill on her charge card. A few weeks later, I found out that she submitted the bill from that lunch on her expense account. That seems so wrong, I mean, we paid for the lunch and now she's claimed it on her expenses. I'm really mad about it, but what can I do?

3 1c   2c   3a

16.3

1

Words in the blanks are in *italics*.

By the year 2010, I *expect* that the situation of women in work will have changed dramatically. Already in Britain there are a growing number of women doctors and lawyers, and I'm *sure* that growth in these fields will continue. Women have traditionally been confined to clerical jobs – 'women's work' such as secretarial jobs. But this is changing. It's *likely* that we will see more men doing these jobs in future as women move into managerial and executive positions. It's *unlikely* that by 2010 there will be any idea of men's or women's jobs, whoever is best at a job will be the one who gets it. And I'm *certain* that this means a big change in the job market for women.

2 1b   2d   3c   4e   5a (some variation is possible)

Unit 17

17.1

1 Tick statements 2, 4 and 5
1 The sulphur content is lower.
3 Waste water goes into tanks on the ship but is purified on shore.
6 All the fluids are environmentally friendly, 90 per cent of each fluid is biodegradable.

Stena Line has been listening to the public's concern about the environment. We thought that it would be a good idea to make our ships more environmentally friendly, and we have done this in cooperation with the World Wide Fund for Nature. For example, people suggested reducing the sulphur content of ships' fuel. We have done this, and the sulphur content is now 0.6 per cent. People also said we should pump waste water from kitchens and toilets into a tank. Now, waste water is stored for purification when the boat reaches land instead of being pumped into the sea.

Many suggested separating glass and aluminium packaging for recycling and replacing disposable materials with environmentally friendly alternatives. Quite a few people felt that we should look at the cleaning fluids that are used. We did this, and 146 chemical preparations are no longer used. Those that still are used are all 90 per cent biodegradable.

2 B: That's a good idea.
A: I think we should encourage people to travel to work by bus. How do you feel about this?
B: I don't think that's a very good idea. It takes too long.

17.2

1 1a: *say* + direct quotation   2b: suggest + verb+*ing*
3b: *tell* + object   4a: point out that + verb+*ing*
5b: recommend + verb+*ing*   6a: agree to + verb

2 1a   2c   3b   4a   5c

CHAIR: At our last meeting, we talked about packaging for our new bath oil. Laura, can you tell us what you found out about glass bottles?
LAURA: Yes, of course. I contacted our regular supplier, and they can provide glass bottles that are just slightly more expensive than the present plastic bottles. I contacted several other suppliers, and the prices are pretty much the same. I think it would be a good idea to keep to our present supplier as they have always been helpful.
CHAIR: Thank you Laura. What do you think, James?
JAMES: I really think that using glass is a mistake. We've just heard that it is more expensive, and I still think that plastic is going to be more convenient.
CHAIR: Max, you look like you have an opinion on this.
MAX: James, convenience isn't everything! We want this bath oil to have a more upmarket image. I'm sure that we can find a way of using glass bottles, and I still feel that they are easier to recycle.
CHAIR: Laura, what did you find out about recycling?
LAURA: Our present supplier is happy to take back empty bottles, and the refund on these makes glass very competitive with the price of plastic. I suggest using glass bottles as the price is going to be nearly the same and it will look better.
JAMES: But I still …

3 2 Laura told them / said that she had contacted several suppliers and that the prices were pretty much the same.

3 James said that using glass was a mistake.

4 Max pointed out that convenience wasn't everything.

5 Laura suggested using glass bottles as the price was nearly the same.

17.3

1 2a 3b 4c 5e

2 Beep 1: 2   Beep 2: 3   Beep 3: 1   Beep 4: 5

CHAIR:	Is everyone here? OK, (beep). We're here to discuss ways in which we can reduce expenses. Sandra has a few ideas which she'd like to tell us about.
SANDRA:	Thank you. Yes, I've been trying to find areas where we could save money. I'd like to start by looking at the budget from last year and where we overspent. For example, the entertainment budget was overspent by £10,500–
MARK:	(beep) How can we get business if we don't spend money?
CHAIR:	Sorry, Mark, (beep).
SANDRA:	My next point was that the Sales budget was overspent by £42,500–
JOAN:	(beep) I think Mark's right. We need to spend money to get business.
SANDRA:	Can I just finish? In both cases, we obviously need to spend more money–
MARK/JOAN:	Yes!
SANDRA:	But there does have to be some control. I suggest …

3 Suggested answers

CHAIR (1): As you know, we're here to discuss ways of making the office more green. Paola has some suggestions she would like to make.

CHAIR (2): Just a minute, Richard. We'll talk about these ideas later. Sorry, Paola, please continue.

CHAIR (3): Can we keep to the point? Paola, please continue.

CHAIR (4): Can we move on to the next point?

CHAIR (5): Let's not get sidetracked. Paola, any other points?

Unit 18

18.1

1 1 must   2 can   3 cannot   4 mustn't
5 don't have to

3

18.2

1 1e   2d   3f   4c   5a   6b

Nike, the American sports shoe supplier, has reached the top by keeping quality high and costs low. A main ingredient is Asian manufacturing know-how.

This is how Nike works. At the company's headquarters in Beaverton, Oregon, the designers develop shoes for the next season. There are 1,000 models of shoes in Nike's product range and over 100 types are introduced each season.

The designs are then sent by satellite to contractors' computers in Taiwan. Here the blueprints are developed into prototype shoes that can be made on a production line. The plans are then faxed to manufacturing companies in South Korea and engineers in both countries work out how to manufacture shoes dreamed up in America. The shoes are produced at the contractors' factories around the region.

Almost half of Nike's shoes are manufactured by just six companies, three from South Korea and three from Taiwan. These companies have established factories in their own countries and in other Asian countries. In 1992 Nike bought 42 per cent of its shoes from South Korea and 44 per cent from China, Indonesia and Thailand.

2 1 Coffee beans are collected by the farmers.
2 The beans are dried in the sun.
3 The beans are roasted in ovens.
4 The beans are sorted by workers.
5 Bags are packed by machine.
6 Bags are transported to market by sea.

3 First   Next / Then   Then / Next   Finally

18.3

1 1b 2c 3a 4b 5a

2 2 was applied
3 were designed
4 was named
5 was loved
6 was advertised

3

Volvo cars was founded in 1927. In the 1930s Volvo cars were not influenced by design outside Sweden. In 1939 the Carioco was launched. In the 1950s Volvos became popular in the United States. In 1957 Volvo produced a car with safety belts as standard. In the 1960s a TV series provided good publicity.

Unit 19

19.1

1 1d 2c 3b 4a 5e

Hello, Lee, this is Mike. You asked for advice about the organization of the sales conference. We've already decided to hold it in Bangkok, so you need to find out about hotels and the best dates for availability. Once you have this, you should let those who will be coming have details of when it is taking place so they can let you know to book rooms. At this time you should ask delegates if they have any problems or preferences, for example, are there any vegetarians. Then you need to think about the conference schedule – what needs to happen when. Along with the main programme, you need to have a social programme so that people can relax and get to know each other. Finally, prepare the information packs for the participants – they'll need things like the programme, new marketing leaflets, information about Bangkok, things like that. If you need any more help, please let me know.

2 Suggested answer

FAX

To: Central Plaza Hotel, Bangkok
From: Ocean Sound

Message

I am writing to confirm the following details of our Sales Conference.

We would like to book the large conference room for 15 to 17 June. We would also like to book the private dining room for 14 to 17 June. We will have a Welcome dinner on 14 June. We will need 5 double rooms and 17 single rooms for 14 to 18 June.

All 27 participants are arriving the day before the conference starts.

Please let me know if you have any questions about these details or if there are any problems.

3 Suggested answer

OCEAN SOUND

Dear

I am pleased to invite you to this year's Sales Conference. It will be held at the Central Plaza Hotel, Bangkok, on 15 to 17 June.

There will be a Welcome dinner on the night of 14 June, and your rooms have been reserved for the nights of 14 to 17 June.

The Central Plaza Hotel is situated in the heart of Bangkok. The hotel is organizing a tour of the Grand Palace on the night of 15 June, and on the night of 16 June there will be a dance at the hotel for participants.

If there are any problems, please write to the Conference Coordinator, Lee Bristow.

I look forward to seeing you at the conference!

19.2

1

June 15	June 16
Director's Welcome and Annual Report	New products 3: KF5000
Coffee	*Coffee*
New products 1: KK90	New products 4: KL6000
Break	*Break*
New products 2: KS300	New marketing strategies 2
Lunch	*Lunch*
New marketing strategies 1	Report on this year's sales
Tea	*Tea*
Regional reports	Plans for next year
Dinner: Presentation of Sales Awards	*Dinner*
Tour of the Grand Palace	*Dance*

2 1T   2F (after lunch)   3F   4T

This is the Director. Thanks for making those changes to the conference programme. I'm afraid I've still got a few problems. One of our most important sales people has to leave at lunch time on 16 June. Unfortunately, she was going to present the Report on this year's sales. So that session had better be on 15 June, the last session of the day. Regional reports can then be after lunch on 16 June. The other problem is that the tour for 15 June has been cancelled. I think it would be better anyway to have the dance after the awards are presented, so could you arrange that, please? Could you also see what other activity we could do after dinner on 16 June? Thanks.

19.3

1 1 Ocean Sound produces sound software for computers.
2 The sound schemes allow you to personalize your computer to make computing more enjoyable.
3 The advantages of the KL6000 are that it offers faster processing and high quality sound reproduction.

4 a Miniature sound effects will allow good sound quality for even the smallest hand-held games.   b Improved electronic voices will give computer voices that sound nearly like you.

2 Suggested answer

Welcome to this year's Ocean Sound Sales Conference. I'm glad that you could all come to Bangkok, and I'm sure that you will have an interesting time.

I am the Director of Ocean Sound, and I would like to tell you something about the company and our new products.

Ocean Sound was founded 25 years ago. From the start we produced sound software for computers. Our sound schemes make computing more enjoyable because computer users can personalize their sound schemes. These schemes also help people who have problems with their eyesight use computers.

New developments for this year include the KL6000. As the computer games market has grown, we have aimed to supply top quality sound effects. This new software provides fast processing and high quality sound to make games more realistic. The life-like graphics are now matched by life-like sounds.

Once again, thank you for coming to the conference, and I hope that you will have an enjoyable time.

Progress test 4

20.1

1 made
2 have fallen
3 lost
4 have decided
5 said
6 told
7 have reached

20.2

1 I need a new assistant.
2 I suggest we hire someone who speaks several languages.
3 Could you write the advertisement, please?
4 Gina said that she needed a new computer.
5 Rolando suggested that she needed the DX2000 model.
6 Maria asked how much they cost.

20.3

Suggested answers

1 You must not smoke in the office.
2 You can eat lunch anytime between 12 and 2.
3 You don't have to finish work at 5.
4 You have to work 42 hours a week.
5 You cannot make personal calls.
6 You can start work at 7.30.

20.4

1 Letters were typed by secretaries.
2 The computer was invented by Alan Turing.
3 The body is welded to the frame by robots.
4 Orders are sent by E-mail.
5 Machines harvest cotton.
6 Ships took cargoes around the world.
7 Robots assemble cars.

20.5

1a 2b 3c 4c 5b

MIKE: Barbara, I've just been reading a report on a survey of business ethics in this magazine. I know you've got to go soon, but do you want to try the first two questions?

BARBARA: Sure.

MIKE: OK, first question. Which of these companies would you work for: a nuclear waste disposal company, a company with a bad pollution record, or a company that exploits Third World countries.

BARBARA: Really, I wouldn't want to work for any of them!

MIKE: OK, but pick the company that is the least bad!

BARBARA: Well, then I suppose it would be the company with the bad pollution record. The others make their money out of activities I don't approve of. At least the company with the bad pollution record might change!

MIKE: Fine. Question two. A colleague of yours makes calls while at work to family and friends all around the world. He says that he makes a lot of money for the company, so the company owes him something. Do you agree with his attitude?

BARBARA: No! A company pays you for the work you do. That is the agreement.

MIKE: OK. Do you want to hear the results from these two questions?

BARBARA: Let's hear them.

MIKE: For question one, 45 per cent of people said they'd rather work for the nuclear disposal company, 38 per cent said they'd work for the company with the pollution record, and 17 per cent said they'd work for the company that exploited the Third World. For question two, 80 per cent of people did not agree with the employee's attitude, while 15 per cent agreed and 5 per cent had no opinion. But women were …